The Champion of Paribanou

A Play

Alan Ayckbourn

A SAMUEL FRENCH ACTING EDITION

FOUNDED 1830

SAMUELFRENCH-LONDON.CO.UK
SAMUELFRENCH.COM

ISBN 978-0-573-05123-4

www.samuelfrench-london.co.uk

www.samuelfrench.com

FOR AMATEUR PRODUCTION ENQUIRIES

UNITED KINGDOM AND WORLD
EXCLUDING NORTH AMERICA
plays@SamuelFrench-London.co.uk
020 7255 4302/01

Each title is subject to availability from Samuel French,

depending upon country of performance.

THE CHAMPION OF PARIBANOU

First performed at the Stephen Joseph Theatre, Scarborough, on 29th November, 1996. The cast was as follows:

The Sultan	Malcolm Rennie
Houssain	Andrew Mallett
Ali	Howard Saddler
Ahmed	Jonathan McGuiness
The Grand Vizier	Adrian McLoughlin
Murganah	Pauline Turner
Princess Nouronnihar	Eleanor Tremain
Safia	Kate Farrah
Salim	Colin Gourley
Highwayman	Malcolm Rennie
Schaibar	Colin Gourley
Innkeeper	Wolf Christian
Paribanou	Kate Farrah
Nasuh	Wolf Christian

Directed by **Alan Ayckbourn**
Design by **Roger Glossop**
Costume Design by **Elaine Garrard**
Lighting by **Mick Hughes**
Fight Director **Wolf Christian**
Music by **John Pattison**

CHARACTERS

The Sultan
Houssain, the Sultan's first son
Ali, the Sultan's second son
Ahmed, the Sultan's third son
The Grand Vizier
Murganah, the Grand Vizier's daughter
Nouronnihar, a princess
Safia, Nouronnihar's maid
Salim, Nouronnihar's father's emissary
Paribanou
Nasuh, Paribanou's servant
Schaibar, the stranger
Highwayman
Innkeeper

Suggested doubles:

Safia and **Paribanou**
Schaibar and **Salim**
Innkeeper and **Nasuh**
Highwayman and **Sultan**

A land in the forgotten past or the undreamt future

ACT I

Scene 1

The Sultan's Palace Grounds

The Vizier enters in a hurry. He is elderly and rather flustered

Vizier (*calling*) My Lord Houssain! My Lord! Prince Houssain!

Houssain appears from high up, as if in a tree. He has been reading a book. He is the lean, rather scholarly one of the Sultan's three sons

Houssain Hallo? Somebody want me?
Vizier My Lord Houssain! Please!
Houssain What's the problem?
Vizier My Lord, it's noon.
Houssain (*unconcerned, gazing at the sky*) Good heavens! So it must be.
Vizier Thursday.
Houssain Right.
Vizier The third month of the second moon...
Houssain Thank you so much for reminding me, Grand Vizier. Good day to you.
Vizier My Lord, please, the Princess...
Houssain Princess?
Vizier ...arrives in a few minutes. Your father is expecting you and your brothers in the palace at noon to greet her on her arrival. This has been arranged for weeks. For months. For years. The clock has just struck twelve *and not one of you is there*! NOW PLEASE!
Houssain Oh. You mean Princess...
Vizier ...Her Highness the Princess Nouronnihar...
Houssain ...Nouronnihar. Quite. Couldn't she just ... meet the others...? I've... I've got a lot of reading...
Vizier (*imploringly*) My Lord!
Houssain All right, I'm coming. Princess Nouronnihar... Oh, if there's one thing I loathe it's princesses... (*He starts to climb down from the tree*)
Vizier Do you know where your brothers are, my Lord?
Houssain Haven't the faintest idea. If you're looking for Prince Ali, I should start in the maids' quarters...

Houssain exits

Vizier (*muttering to himself*) The maids' quarters… Why didn't I think of that? The maids' quarters… of course! (*He moves on*) The maids' quarters. (*He calls up to a window*) Prince Ali! My Lord! Prince Ali!

Ali appears at the window, shirtless. He is the good-looking, well-built and (it has to be said) rather vain brother

Ali Shhh! Quietly! You'll wake her husband!
Vizier Her husband!
Ali Only joking… What do you want, it's only—first thing in the morning…
Vizier It is noon on the Thursday of the third month of the second moon…
Ali Thanks very much. Goodbye! (*He makes to withdraw*)
Vizier My Lord…
Maid (*off, sleepily*) Ali…
Ali (*to the Vizier*) Cheerio!
Vizier …please…
Maid (*off*) …come back to bed…
Ali Coming, my love…
Vizier The Princess Nouronnihar!
Ali (*puzzled*) The Princess Nouronnihar?
Vizier The Princess Nouronnihar.
Ali Oh, that Princess Nouronnihar. Arrived, has she?
Vizier Imminently. Your father is awaiting you.
Ali Well, tell him—can't you tell him I'm…?
Vizier No, my Lord. *You* tell him. He'll probably only have you beaten; me, he'll execute!
Ali Good thinking. I'll just get my shirt.
Vizier Please, where pray is your younger brother?
Ali Ahmed? Who knows. In the clouds? Dreaming? Playing his life away? I'll tell you what, though … wherever your daughter is—he won't be far away… Find Murganah, you'll have found Ahmed. Bet you! (*He withdraws his head. To someone inside*) Alas, my love! I have to go…
Maid (*off, disappointedly*) Oh! Ali!

Ali goes

The Vizier moves on

Vizier (*annoyed with himself*) Find Murganah, you'll find Prince Ahmed. Where else! (*He calls as he goes*) Murganah! Where are you, girl? Murganah!

The Vizier goes off. As he does so, two figures appear. They are fighting with practice swords. Both are wearing protective helmets so are indistinguishable. One is the boyish figure of Murganah. She is young and athletic and clearly the superior fighter. Her opponent, Ahmed, is furiously defending himself. It is good-natured, almost playful as Murganah toys with him

Murganah (*inviting Ahmed to attack her*) Yes? Come on ... come on...

Ahmed falls for the trick and makes a lunge at her. She twists away, easily evading him. Ahmed loses his balance and falls over

Ahmed Aaah! Not again...

Murganah disarms him

Every time!

She holds her sword above him as if to make the final coup de grâce

Murganah And ... die!
Ahmed (*rather overdoing it*) Aaaarrrrhhh! Aaaarrrggghhh! Ugghh!

Murganah takes off her helmet and sits on the ground beside him now, laughing and laying aside her sword

Murganah You never learn, do you?
Ahmed I'm hopeless, hopeless... Every time. Same old trick. I've never won. Not once.
Murganah Lucky you have me to look after you then, isn't it?
Ahmed Yes, but I'm... That's the problem. I'm supposed to look after you...
Murganah Who says?
Ahmed Well, it's a fact. I'm the man. I'm supposed to look after you.
Murganah Because I'm the woman?
Ahmed Yes.
Murganah Why can't the woman look after the man?
Ahmed I don't know. They just don't. They're not supposed to. I'm supposed to look after you. That's the way it is.
Murganah But you can't look after me, can you?
Ahmed I know.
Murganah You're useless.
Ahmed That's the problem.
Murganah So I'll have to look after you then, won't I?

Ahmed (*a little unhappily*) Yes. Thank you.
Murganah For ever.
Ahmed Yes.
Murganah As blood twins.
Ahmed Yes.
Murganah No-one else?
Ahmed No.
Murganah Ever?
Ahmed No.
Murganah Swear?
Ahmed (*hesitating*) I can't.
Murganah You won't?
Ahmed I'm a prince...
Murganah So?
Ahmed Princes have to—there's things they have to do. They can't always choose.
Murganah Why not?
Ahmed You know why. It's the way it is... We're not free. None of us are.
Murganah I am. I'm free. I obey nobody. I am answerable to no-one but myself.
Ahmed No, you're not. You're the Grand Vizier's daughter, you have as much responsibility as anyone else. You're——
Murganah I'm not his daughter. I'm adopted.
Ahmed Nonetheless...
Murganah I'm a child of the forest. I told you. I was abandoned by wolves. My mother found me wrapped in tiger skins, hidden under the leaves. I was wild like an animal...
Ahmed Murganah!
Murganah What?
Ahmed Come on. We don't know this for certain.
Murganah I do. (*She looks at him for a second*) Ahmed, do you love me?
Ahmed (*hesitatingly*) Yes...
Murganah I love you.
Ahmed I know.
Murganah Then what else can matter?

She stands defiantly

   (*Yelling*) Let them all come. I'm ready for you!

   The Vizier enters

Vizier Murganah!

Murganah (*startled*) Father!

Vizier What are you playing at? Look at the way you're dressed! Look at your clothes. You're a disgrace. What on earth do you think you're doing, girl? If your step-mother was alive she'd drop dead with shame.

Murganah What's wrong?

Vizier You know perfectly well. I've told you a hundred times. You're not a child any more, you're a grown woman, Murganah. So try and behave like one and not like a street urchin.

Murganah How do you know? Maybe I am a street urchin. How do you know what I am?

Vizier That's enough! My Lord Ahmed, the Princess Nouronnihar is arriving at any minute. Your father says will you please assemble with your brothers in the Grand Drawing-Room immediately.

Ahmed Goodness, is that today?

Vizier (*wearily*) My Lord, you knew it was today. Twelve noon on the Thursday of the third month of the second moon. I wrote it down for you...

Ahmed Oh, yes.

Vizier And Murganah. I've arranged for you to attend on the Princess as her maidservant during her stay here.

Murganah Attend on her? Me?

Vizier Yes. It's about time you learnt something useful, girl. Up to your room and get changed. Come along both of you, please. Hurry! Please!

The Vizier goes

Murganah (*in a fury*) I'm not attending on her. I'm not a servant. How dare he! Who does he think I am?

Ahmed (*gently*) Murganah!

Murganah I'm nobody's servant! I'm me! I'm free!

Ahmed Murganah... We all have a role to play. I have one and so do you.

Murganah Oh, Ahmed... (*She suddenly clings to him, tearfully*) What's going to happen to us, Ahmed?

Ahmed I don't know.

Murganah You'll marry this princess, I know it...

Ahmed (*surprised*) What?

Murganah You'll see her and fall straight in love with her. I know you will.

Ahmed Nonsense. I'm not marrying a princess...

Murganah Then why is she here?

Ahmed I don't know.

Murganah To arrange a marriage. Why else do princesses come visiting?

Ahmed Well, what if she is? I don't care. If she wants to marry someone, let her. She can marry Ali or Houssain...

Murganah And what if she prefers you? What if she wants to marry you?

Ahmed I'll tell her, no, thank you.

Murganah No, you won't. Because you're not free. You've said so. You'll have to marry her, won't you? And then what's going to happen to us? To me? Heaven knows where I came from. Heaven knows where I'm going.

Ahmed Murganah. You always told me—courage. When I was scared, when we were both very little. At night. In the dark. When you were brave for both of us. Courage! Remember?

Murganah (*dully*) Yes.

Ahmed Then, courage. Come on. (*He makes to move off*)

Murganah Ahmed, I'll tell you one thing. If another tries to take you from me, I will kill her. I swear it. You are my blood twin and no-one will ever part us. Ever. I'll die first.

He stares at her

I mean it, Ahmed.

Ahmed (*sadly*) I hope you don't. Come on.

Ahmed goes

Murganah (*to herself, holding up her sword as a cross*) I swear.

As Murganah follows him, the scene changes

SCENE 2

The Grand Drawing-Room in the Sultan's Palace

Houssain and Ali, now more formally dressed, are waiting. Ali is looking out of the window. Houssain is reading his book

Ali They're just arriving. She's getting out of her carriage.

Houssain (*without looking up*) Good.

Ali I can't see what she looks like. She's all—covered up. Probably as plain as a pig. They're greatly over-rated, princesses. In my experience. Give me a kitchen maid any day.

Houssain Or preferably several.

Ali Jealous? I can't help it if women find me irresistible, can I?

Houssain My dear chap, you're welcome to all the women in the world. All I want is to settle down with a good book. Only people keep interrupting.

Ali How can you possibly read at a time like this? Our whole future's at stake. One of us is going to have to marry her. (*He continues to look out*)

Houssain Not me.
Ali Well, certainly not me.
Houssain Lucky old Ahmed, then.
Ali (*laughing*) If she wants Ahmed, she'll have to deal with Murganah first. Don't fancy anyone's chances there. Hey, she's got this huge man with her. Must be her bodyguard... Father's greeting them... (*He mimics his father*) Pray welcome, princess, to our humble palace. All three hundred and twenty-seven rooms...

A fanfare

Look out! They're coming. Is my hair all right?

Ahmed enters, struggling into his jacket

Houssain Come on, Ahmed. Where have you been?
Ali Playing soldiers with Murganah. I bet she beat you as usual.
Ahmed Possibly she did.
Ali Possibly she did. You couldn't beat a blind tortoise...
Houssain Leave him alone, Ali...

The Vizier enters, hurriedly

Vizier Quickly, now. They're here, they're here!

Another fanfare

The Sultan enters, escorting the Princess Nouronnihar. The Sultan is elderly, but impressive and incisive. A no-nonsense military man. Nouronnihar is followed in turn by Safia, her silent maid. We see little of Nouronnihar at first as both women are heavily veiled. Safia is to remain so throughout. Following them is Salim, the Princess's escort. He is, as described, a giant. Armoured, metallic, menacing and, as we are soon to discover, non-human, mechanical and slightly faulty

The Princes bow to the Princess. Nouronnihar curtsies to the sons in turn

Sultan May I first of all welcome you, Princess Nouronnihar, to our humble palace...
Ali (*muttering*) All three hundred and twenty-seven rooms...
Sultan (*with a sharp look at Ali*) And to introduce my three sons. Houssain, my eldest. Ali, my second son. And finally Ahmed, my youngest.
Nouronnihar (*formally*) I greet you all.

Houssain The pleasure is ours, Princess, I assure you.
Ali I am utterly enchanted, Princess. I am yours to serve.
Ahmed Hi!
Sultan My youngest, as you observe, Princess, is still a boy. (*He glares at Ahmed*)
Nouronnihar Surely not? To me he seems every inch a man.
Ahmed (*pleased*) Thank you very much. (*He smiles at her, gratefully*)
Nouronnihar May I in turn introduce Salim, my escort and Emissary of my father, The Imperial Grand Ruler of Kawar and All its Environs. Salim brings greetings from my father and a message of friendship from the people of The Glorious Kingdom of Kawar. Salim! Speak the message.

Salim gives a sudden shudder and starts to deliver the message

Salim Grook oorrr crake bying bong orse rrok bikk sprak soot wick bike toong ding rooot speckle ting coke...
Ahmed (*to Ali*) What's he saying?
Ali No idea...
Salim ...harder creck creck sprenkle tack-tack-tack-tack-tack... (*He appears to have got stuck*)

Nouronnihar hits him with the flat of her hand

(*Triumphantly*) Tacker-rackar! (*He gives a gurgle and stops*)
Vizier Bravo. A most—moving and eloquent message.

Salim gives another gurgle

Sultan I wonder if he'd mind saying that all again.
Nouronnihar I believe that would be difficult. Salim is, of course, mechanical.
Sultan (*startled*) Mechanical. Good gracious!
Nouronnihar On our way here we encountered several thunderstorms. He has become extremely rusty.
Vizier Perhaps some oil. (*He calls*) Oil for the Emissary!
Sultan If I may be permitted, Grand Vizier...
Vizier I am sorry, sire...
Sultan We can oil him later. To the point of our meeting today. We are all of us aware that in the past there have been some differences between your father, Princess, and myself. Between our own State and that of the Kingdom of Kawar there has been an unfortunate tension. Today it is our hope that through a union of our respective children, by means of the marriage of the Princess Nouronnihar with one of my sons, we shall build a new bridge of friendship and co-operation between our two peoples.

Vizier Hear! Hear!

Salim makes a grinding noise by way of consent. Nouronnihar hits him. He stops

Nouronnihar It is indeed my father's dearest wish that this may be achieved. And, of course, my own.
Sultan As it is my sons'. Boys?
Houssain Yes.
Ali Oh, yes.
Ahmed You bet.
Sultan It is for you to choose, Princess. The choice is yours. Take your time. You are welcome to stay as long as you wish. Get acquainted with them all. Although as a father I am possibly a little biased—may I say that I don't feel that any one of them will disappoint you.
Nouronnihar I am certain they will not. The choice will be very hard for me. Would you... Would you permit me, sire, to have a word alone with your sons?
Sultan Of course. (*Roguishly*) The heart is impatient, eh?
Nouronnihar (*coyly*) I fear it is, sire.
Sultan Oh, I understand. I too was young once. Believe it or not. (*He laughs*)
Ali (*laughing, to the others*) A likely story.
Nouronnihar (*laughing*) Oh, I do. I do believe it, sire.
Sultan Come, Vizier, let us leave these young people. I'm sure we can trust them to behave. Vizier, while they are talking, tell the kitchens to prepare a feast for a hundred people. And a drop of our finest oil for the Emissary.

Salim makes a grinding noise

I will see you at the feast, Princess.
Nouronnihar (*curtsying*) I look forward to it eagerly, sire.

The Sultan goes. Followed by the Vizier, and Salim, who initially has trouble finding the door

An awkward silence

Houssain Princess, before you jump to any...
Ali ...hasty...
Ahmed ...conclusions...
Houssain Make up your mind...
Ali Too fast...
Ahmed We ought to tell you...

Nouronnihar Listen, all of you. We need to talk... (*She pulls at her veil*) Oh,
hang on, I can't talk in this thing... (*She takes off her veil, to reveal herself
a pretty but determined young woman, very used to having things her own
way*) That's better. Now. We haven't much time. I take it you don't want
this marriage, any of you? Any more than I do?
Houssain Well...
Nouronnihar Do you?
Ahmed No.
Ali Sorry, but——
Nouronnihar Don't be sorry. I certainly don't. When I get married, I need
a better reason than this, I can tell you. To hell with my father. I'll marry
who I want to marry and it certainly won't be one of you.
Ali (*slightly hurt*) Ah!
Nouronnihar So, what are we going to do? I take it your father will not be
too pleased if you simply said no?
Houssain No.
Ali What about your father?
Nouronnihar My father? He'd probably have me executed.
Ahmed Really?
Nouronnihar He had my sister executed for refusing to finish her tea. He's
not the most forgiving of men...
Houssain What are we going to do, then?

A silence

Ahmed I have a thought. What if—what if you said that we were all so—
undesirable that you didn't want any of us?
Nouronnihar I don't think that would solve anything. They'd simply say,
bad luck, you'll just have to choose the one you hate the least.
Ali No, that wouldn't work. They'd never believe that you hated me.
Nouronnihar (*coolly*) Really? Fancy yourself, do you?
Ali Doesn't everyone?
Ahmed What if—what if you said you'd fallen in love with all of us, then?
Nouronnihar Why? What good would that do?
Ahmed Just an idea...
Nouronnihar No, wait. It might work. What if you were all madly in love
with me as well? Then—we would have to solve it—with a—with a what?
Ali With a quest. We three would have to go on a quest.
Houssain They always do in the books.
Nouronnihar Right.
Ahmed A quest for what?
Nouronnihar It doesn't really matter—something...
Houssain ...something difficult...

Ali ...something impossible...

Houssain That could take forever to find. Well, five years, anyway...

Ali Seven years...

Ahmed Ten years...

Nouronnihar For as long as they'll let us. Yes, this is good. I want each of you to find me—a—let's see—an object from beyond my wildest dreams. How about that?

Houssain Wonderful.

Ali Difficult.

Ahmed That ought to take some finding.

Nouronnihar But, wait... When you return, I shall find all your gifts unsuitable. You will have found nothing to please me.

Houssain Brilliant!

Nouronnihar Better make sure you don't.

Ahmed Then what happens?

Nouronnihar Then you'll all have to go on another quest. We can keep it going for years.

Houssain Inspired!

Nouronnihar One thing, though. This must remain a secret between the four of us. If anyone for a moment suspects that this is simply a deception—that we're not doing this because of our passionate love for each other, then we're done for. We must tell nobody.

Houssain Nobody.

Ali Nobody.

Ahmed Nobody at all?

Nouronnihar Nobody.

Ahmed Ah.

Nouronnihar See you don't. Or we're all dead. Are we sworn?

Houssain Sworn.

Ali Sworn.

Ahmed (*after a hesitation*) Sworn.

Nouronnihar Call them back, then. Let us hope they'll agree to the scheme.

Houssain goes to the door. Nouronnihar replaces her veil

Houssain (*calling*) Hallo, there! We've finished.

The Vizier enters. He is accompanied by Murganah, now dressed for her maidservant duties

Vizier You've decided? Already?

Nouronnihar No. I fear we have suddenly run up against a problem.

Vizier Really? Oh dear.

Nouronnihar It appears this has been a case of love at first sight.

Vizier Indeed. How magical. Between whom and whom, may I enquire?

Nouronnihar Between all of us.

Vizier (*rather taken aback*) All of you?

Nouronnihar (*indicating Houssain*) Between him and me...

Houssain And me and her...

Nouronnihar (*indicating Ali*) And him and me...

Ali And me and her...

Nouronnihar (*indicating Ahmed*) And him and me...

Ahmed (*after a quick look at Murganah*) And me and her...

Vizier Good heavens. But you've only been in here—five minutes. Surely...?

Nouronnihar Ah, but love does not wait, Grand Vizier. It swoops. It pounces, like a cat...

Houssain Like an eagle...

Ali Like a leopard...

Ahmed Like a duck...

Vizier (*uncertainly*) Yes. Well, this is very difficult. What are we to do? You can't all—marry each other. It wouldn't be—proper.

Nouronnihar We have a scheme.

Vizier You do?

Houssain We do.

Vizier What sort of scheme?

Ali We're going on a quest...

Ahmed Different quests.

Houssain We three.

Nouronnihar To find me something beyond my wildest dreams. He who finds the most magical, desirable object will retain my undying love...

Vizier I see. Yes, that's certainly a solution... How long do you think this quest might take?

Ahmed Ten years...

Vizier Oh, no...

Houssain Seven years...

Vizier No, no...

Ali Five years...

Vizier No, no, no... Your father will never agree to that.

Houssain How long do you think, then?

Vizier I should imagine one year. Maximum.

Ali One year?

Ahmed Oh.

Nouronnihar May I speak with the Sultan, Grand Vizier? I will plead for longer...

Houssain No, we'll speak to him.

Ali We know how to get round Father...
Ahmed We'll talk him round.
Nouronnihar (*doubtfully*) Are you sure?
Houssain Leave it to us. (*To the others*) Follow me. All my love, princess,
  is for you...
Ali For you...
Ahmed (*with a glance at Murganah*) For you.
Houssain Farewell! My love!

Houssain exits

Ali Farewell! My precious!

Ali exits

Ahmed (*making to leave*) Farewell! My ... dear!
Murganah (*softly to Ahmed, making to leave*) I'll kill her...
Ahmed (*softly, to Murganah*) No...
Murganah (*to Ahmed*)...and I'll kill you...
Ahmed ...you don't understand...
Nouronnihar (*sharply*) Who is that person there?
Vizier Ah, Princess, this is my daughter—my adopted daughter, Murganah,
  who will be honoured to serve you during your stay here...

Ali enters

Ali (*to Ahmed*) Come on...

Ahmed reluctantly leaves with Ali

Nouronnihar That is to be my servant...?
Vizier She would deem it an honour...
Nouronnihar Then I would deem it an honour if she were properly dressed.
Vizier Is there something wrong with her dress?
Nouronnihar Why isn't she veiled? In my country a servant is veiled at all
  times when in the presence of her mistress in order to let her mistress's
  beauty shine unchallenged... Pull on your veil, girl, at once.
Murganah I'm not putting on——
Vizier (*sharply*) Murganah! (*More quietly*) Do as you're told.
Murganah Father, I cannot serve her. If you make me serve her—I promise
  I'll—I can't!
Vizier Excuse me, Princess. (*He draws Murganah aside, gently*) It is time
  you learnt to serve, Murganah. You cannot play for ever, child. You're

grown up now. Like everyone else in the world, you have duties. For the
next few months your duty is to the Princess. You will obey her every
command. And devote yourself to her. Do you understand that?

Murganah bows her head

Murganah (*almost inaudibly*) Yes...
Vizier Good. Now, do as she commands.

Murganah pulls up her veil obediently

Princess, my daughter is happy and willing to serve you. Please forgive her
indiscretion.
Nouronnihar Of course, Grand Vizier.
Vizier If you will excuse me, I must attend the Sultan and see what has been
decided. I think I may have to cancel that feast. Until the happy day!
Nouronnihar Until the happy day!
Vizier Incidentally, Princess, your Emissary—Salim. He's—he's just
walked through the wall of the dining-room. Never mind. (*He laughs*)
What's a wall here or there, eh?

The Vizier leaves

*Nouronnihar removes her veil and tosses it on the floor. She sighs a little
impatiently*

Nouronnihar Why are all men such fools?
Murganah Not all of them are. There are some who——
Nouronnihar Be quiet! How dare you speak in my presence! How dare you?
Did I ask you to speak? In my country, a servant who speaks out of turn has
her tongue cut out. Do you know that? You speak once more unless you're
spoken to and I'll see that happens to you. Do you hear? I said, do you hear
me?
Murganah (*hissing*) Yes...
Nouronnihar Princess...
Murganah Princess...
Nouronnihar I hope you do. Come along, then. (*She makes to leave with
Safia. To Murganah, indicating her veil*) And pick that up, then! At this rate
you won't last a week.

Nouronnihar leaves with Safia

Murganah pulls back her own veil angrily. She is trembling with anger. She picks up the veil which Nouronnihar has discarded. In a violent motion she tears it in half

Murganah I'm nobody's servant! I'm free!

Murganah goes. As she does so the scene changes

SCENE 3

The Sultan's Palace Courtyard. It is night

The sound of restless horses

The brothers are cloaked and ready to depart

Ali This is a fine time to start on a quest. It's the middle of the night. I've got far better things I could be doing at this time of night.
Houssain You heard what Father said. We start at midnight and we must return at midnight in six months' time.
Ali So much for seven years.
Ahmed So much for ten.
Ali Maybe she'll get fed up with waiting for us and marry someone else whilst we're away.
Ahmed Maybe she'll die.
Ali Maybe we will.
Houssain Let's get the horses...

A light appears at a window. Nouronnihar looks out

Nouronnihar *(calling softly)* Goodbye!
Houssain Goodbye!
Ali See you in six months...
Ahmed Six months! I don't want to leave here for six months.
Nouronnihar Yes, you do. Goodbye! Bring me back something beautiful. Far beyond my wildest dreams...
Houssain We will, we will! I'm off to Bisnager, a city with the largest library in the world.
Ali And I to Persia where the wom... where there's some very nice people, so I've heard.
Ahmed I go to Samarkand, the land of magic and adventure. For a whole six months. On my own.
Houssain Farewell!

Ali Farewell!
Ahmed Goodbye!
Nouronnihar Farewell!

The three men go

(To herself, as she closes the window) I hope you all fall down a deep well, you stupid oafs!

Nouronnihar goes in

The sound of the horses departing

A cloaked, hooded figure slips from the shadows. Although we cannot identify her, it is Murganah. She hesitates, checking the coast is clear and then hurries across the courtyard and off in the direction that the men have taken. As this happens the scene changes

SCENE 4

The Inn in the Distance

A traditional Olde Inne with several tables

At one of these, in a corner, sits Schaibar, dressed in black. His face is always hidden by a deep hood. He pays no attention to the ensuing scene but concentrates on a game of patience he is playing with selected tarot cards

At another table sits the Highwayman. His features, which are visible, are highly unsavoury

In a moment, Ahmed enters

Ahmed Whew! Cold out there! Good evening.

Neither of the other two acknowledge him

Is the landlord...? *(He calls)* Landlord! We've been riding since last night. Hardly stopped. Yes. *(He calls again)* Landlord! My horse is lame. Just a little. She pulled up. Nothing serious. Tired, I think. *(The silence is unnerving him)* Landlord!

The Innkeeper appears. He is almost as evil-looking as the Highwayman

Ah! Landlord! Yes?

Innkeeper Sir! Good sir! I'm so sorry. Can I be of service?

Ahmed Yes. I was just telling these gentlemen ... my horse is lame. I don't think it's serious but if someone could take a look.

Innkeeper Certainly, sir. Certainly. (*With a great yell*) MAXWELL! SEE TO THE MAN'S HORSE! (*In his normal tone*) Maxwell will see to it, sir. Would you care for a seat, whilst you're waiting. Maxwell is magic with horses, sir. He could do anything with them...

Highwayman Stewed, fried, boiled...

Ahmed I'm sorry...

Innkeeper (*laughing*) Ignore that gentleman, sir. Ignore him. He has a wicked humour. Wicked. A glass of fine ale, sir. Something to eat, perhaps?

Ahmed No, I haven't time for anything to eat, but I'd love a glass of ale, thank you.

Innkeeper A pleasure, sir. Have you a long journey ahead, then?

Ahmed Yes, indeed. I have to reach the frontier by dawn. Is it far?

Innkeeper Oh ... a good twenty miles, sir. Long haul in the dark. In these parts. Would you not prefer to spend the night? We have rooms. Capacious rooms. Start fresh in the morning. Much safer, sir. (*To the Highwayman*) Eh?

Highwayman Much safer.

Innkeeper Treacherous round here after dark, sir. (*To the Highwayman*) Eh?

Highwayman Dreadful.

Ahmed Yes. Odd you should say that. We've had this feeling we've been followed. But I'll have to take my chances. I need to catch up with my brothers. They've ridden on ahead.

During the following the Highwayman takes out a long knife

Innkeeper Then you're on your own then, are you, sir?

Ahmed Yes. On my own. Temporarily.

Innkeeper Glass of fine ale, sir?

Ahmed Thank you.

The Innkeeper goes off

(*To the Highwayman*) Nice man.

The Highwayman ignores him. He is intent on cleaning his fingernails with the knife. Ahmed gets up, rather nervously. He wanders over to Schaibar's table. He stares over his shoulder at the cards

Ah, now. Does that card go on...?

Schaibar, with a single, deft movement, turns over a row of face down cards.
They are all identical. The Death Card

(*Nervously*) Ah, no, probably not. Sorry, my mistake. (*He moves away to*
the fire)

The Innkeeper enters with a tankard of ale

Innkeeper Fine ale, sir.
Ahmed Ah, thank you.

The Innkeeper chooses a table with a chair with its back to the Highwayman
upon which to put down the tankard

Innkeeper Here, sir. Out of the draught.
Ahmed Thank you. (*He sits*) How much do I owe you?
Innkeeper Just two grutts, sir…
Ahmed (*groping for his purse*) Two grutts, right. That's very reasonable.
(*He finds his purse*) Here we are. You may have to change a scrone. I don't
think I've got anything smaller.
Innkeeper Oh, that'll be all right, sir. (*He takes the purse out of Ahmed's*
hand) I'll just take this. It'll be a lot easier.

The Highwayman gets up and moves behind Ahmed. Ahmed goes to grab the
purse back. He grabs the Innkeeper's sleeve

Ahmed Wait a minute! You can't do that. Give me that back…

The Highwayman grabs Ahmed's arms

What are you…? What's going on?
Innkeeper (*as they struggle*) The knife… Use your knife.
Highwayman Then hold him, why can't you?

Ahmed kicks out with his feet, catching the Innkeeper in the stomach

Innkeeper Ufff! (*He collapses in a heap, totally winded. He drops the purse*)

Ahmed wriggles free from the Highwayman and grabs back his purse. He
turns to run, but the Highwayman, with the knife in his hand again, has
Ahmed cornered

Highwayman (*brandishing the knife dangerously*) Come on! Give it me,
boy! Come on, then!

Ahmed No.
Highwayman Come on! I'll cut you, else. I'll cut you, boy. Come on.
Ahmed No. It's all the money I have.
Highwayman All right. You asked for it... (*He moves in*)

Suddenly the front door bursts open. A masked figure stands there, sword drawn

The Highwayman turns, startled

Who the...? Who are you?

The figure advances with the sword. Ineffectually, the Highwayman tries to fend off the stranger with his knife. A flick of the sword and he is disarmed, clasping his injured hand

Aaaah! You'll be sorry for that.

Another lunge with the sword. He backs away

All right, then, steady! I'm leaving! I'm leaving! I tell you, I'm leaving! There's no need for that! (*He is backed out of the door*) I'll be back.

The Highwayman exits

The stranger closes the door and turns to Ahmed

Ahmed Sir, I have to thank you. I have no idea who you are, but...

The "stranger" removes her mask. It is Murganah

Murganah!
Murganah Promised I would look after you...
Ahmed How did you get here?
Murganah How else? I followed you.
Ahmed I didn't recognize you. Dressed like that.
Murganah How do you expect me to dress in this part of the country at night? In a silk dress?

The Innkeeper groans

You. Get up. And bring us some more ale.
Innkeeper He attacked me. Why should I bring him ale?

Murganah Because if you don't, I shall attack you.
Innkeeper You? Who are you?
Murganah Someone who doesn't like cheats or thieves and has been known
to kill them on sight. Ale! And be quick about it!

The Innkeeper scuttles out

You should take care, Ahmed. Your trouble is you trust everyone and treat
them all as friends.
Ahmed How else am I to behave? Treat them all as enemies?
Murganah No. But you should be careful. Friends are rare. Real friends like
me are precious. Value me, Ahmed. Instead of racing off on quests for
Princesses with less brain than a dead maggot whom you don't even love.
Ahmed How do you know I don't?
Murganah Because I know you. Because you're my blood twin. You can't
love her. Say it if you can. Tell me that you love Nouronnihar, if you dare.
Ahmed (*with difficulty*) I—I love—Nouronnihar.
Murganah (*staring at him quietly*) You're lying!
Ahmed Please, Murganah, turn round and go home...
Murganah You're lying!
Ahmed One day I will explain everything to you——
Murganah You're lying...
Ahmed —but at present I'm sworn to secrecy...
Murganah You're lying! You're lying! You're lying! (*She snatches up the
Highwayman's discarded dagger and holds it to Ahmed's throat*) Tell me
you're lying! If you're telling the truth, I swear I'll kill you, Ahmed.
Ahmed Then you'll have to kill me.

A silence. Murganah withdraws the dagger

(*As calmly as he can*) I have to go now to find my brothers. Please don't
follow us any further. One day you will understand what we are doing. One
day you will forgive me.
Murganah (*softly*) You were my friend. I loved you. I loved you more than
my life. You've betrayed me. You're now my enemy.
Ahmed Murganah, don't——
Murganah Get away from me——
Ahmed Murganah...
Murganah (*with a cry*) Get out!

Ahmed leaves, sadly

(*To herself*) Help me! By all the heavens, by all the darkest forces, by all that guide us by day, by all that seek to destroy us by night, help me! Help me! (*She plunges the knife into the table*)

Schaibar throughout all this has continued calmly with his card game

Schaibar (*without looking up, calmly*) That's no way to treat a good table.
Murganah (*having barely noticed him before, startled*) What?
Schaibar I think you're attacking the wrong thing. That table has done you no harm that I can see.
Murganah Who are you?
Schaibar Oh, just a passing stranger. You seem distressed, child. Have you a problem?
Murganah What is it to you, if I have? Mind your own business.
Schaibar Maybe I can help.
Murganah (*sarcastically*) How? By telling my fortune?
Schaibar Perhaps by shaping your fortune.
Murganah What are you saying? What is this nonsense?
Schaibar You called upon certain powers just now. To help you. Did you not?
Murganah I was—I was upset. I do that.
Schaibar Nonetheless such powers do exist. They're yours to control.
Murganah What powers?
Schaibar Powers such as these... (*He makes a pass with his hand*)

Ahmed appears in an image. He seems to have lost his way

Murganah (*amazed*) Ahmed! Where is he?
Schaibar On his journey. Lost, as usual... (*Softly*) That way, Ahmed, that way...

Ahmed finds his way. The image fades

Murganah By what trickery did you do that?
Schaibar Call it trickery, call it what you will. It can be yours. That's but a tiny fraction of what you can do.
Murganah (*whispering*) Could it give me wealth...?
Schaibar At only the smallest price...
Murganah Could it give me power...?
Schaibar With only the smallest sacrifice...
Murganah Happiness?
Schaibar At the cost of only the briefest tears...
Murganah My every wish?
Schaibar All that your heart secretly craves for...

Murganah Can be mine?

Schaibar Can be yours.

Murganah (*laughing, only half believing him*) Really? But in return? What do I have to give you in return?

Schaibar Yourself.

Murganah Myself? I see. What sort of bargain is that? I give myself to someone whose face I've never seen?

Schaibar You need give nothing now. Only at the end will I come to claim you. And at the end I will also show you my face. I promise.

Murganah The end of what?

Schaibar At the end of your worldly ambition.

Murganah If I have wealth and power and happiness and all that my heart desires, that could be years away...

Schaibar It could indeed. I can wait.

Murganah You may not even be alive.

Schaibar That is my risk.

Murganah considers

Murganah (*still uncertain whether to take it seriously*) Very well. I agree.

Schaibar Are you sure? Once we've sealed the bargain there is no going back.

Murganah I am sure.

Schaibar Then give me your hand.

Murganah removes her gauntlet and places her hand in Schaibar's

> By all the powers in me,
> Where e'er they be,
> I give to thee.

Murganah gives a cry and snatches back her hand

It is done.

Murganah is examining the palm of her hand. There is now a black star imprinted on the palm

Murganah My hand! What have you done to my hand?

Schaibar A keepsake, lest you forget our bargain. Till we meet again, Murganah. Enjoy your life... Use your powers wisely. With them you can build. With them you can equally destroy.

Schaibar goes, melting into the shadows

Murganah When shall I...? (*She glances at her palm*) Nonsense. (*She sees there are three cards left on the table, face down. She turns them over, one by one*) Death ... death ... death... (*Despite herself, she shivers*) Absurd. Right, let us see what we can do with these powers. (*She waves her hand in the manner of Schaibar*)

An image of Nouronnihar appears, similar to the earlier one of Ahmed. Nouronnihar is drinking wine from a glass, laughing and talking silently to someone we cannot see

It works! Well, well, well, Princess. I hope the wine is good. (*She makes another movement of her hand*)

The wine in Nouronnihar's glass changes colour. She sips her drink, unaware that this is happening. She splutters silently and dabs at her mouth with her hand. The wine is evidently now very unpleasant. Murganah laughs with delight. The image fades

Oh, yes! Oh, yes! Oh, Princess, beware. Revenge is sour!

The Innkeeper enters with two tankards on a tray

Innkeeper Sorry about the delay. I had to change the barrel. (*He sees Murganah*) Ah. Where's your friend?
Murganah He's gone. As has the other gentleman.
Innkeeper What other gentleman?
Murganah The one who was sitting there just now.
Innkeeper There was no-one there. Hasn't been all evening. Just you and your friend.
Murganah I see.
Innkeeper Now there's just you, is there? Just you and me. That's cosy. Want to share the ale, then?
Murganah No, you drink it.
Innkeeper Oh, come on. Be a bit friendly.
Murganah I'm going.
Innkeeper Well, you're paying for this, anyway. Might as well drink it.
Murganah I'm not paying. I haven't drunk any.
Innkeeper You ordered it.
Murganah Drink it yourself. Good-night. (*She turns to go*)

The Innkeeper puts down the tray and moves to intercept her

Innkeeper Now just a minute, you're not leaving here till you pay me, one way or the other. Either in money or in kind, I don't care—— (*He makes to grasp her shoulder*)

Murganah turns angrily and with the smallest of gestures sends the man reeling backwards and crashing into a table

(*Winded again*) Ah!
Murganah Good-night.

Murganah goes

The Innkeeper lies on the floor groaning

Innkeeper Oh. I don't think I can get up for six months...

The Lights change to

SCENE 5

The Inn in the Distance. It is a bright sunny morning, six months later

The Innkeeper is staggering to his feet when there is a loud knocking

Houssain (*off; calling*) Innkeeper! Anyone at home?
Innkeeper Just a minute, just a minute. Come in, then.

Houssain enters. He has been travelling. He has a carpet under his arm

Houssain About time. Are you open or closed?
Innkeeper Open. I was—I was asleep.
Houssain Asleep? At eleven o'clock in the morning? You ought to be ashamed of yourself on this fine spring day.
Innkeeper Spring? It's spring?
Houssain Yes, of course it's spring. April.
Innkeeper April.
Houssain Of course April. Bring me some ale.
Innkeeper Yes. (*He examines the two tankards still on the tray*) I'll—get you some fresh. These are rather flat. Been standing a bit.

The Innkeeper goes

Houssain, in a good mood, sings to himself

Ali enters. He carries a telescope

Ali (*as he enters*) Anyone at...? Houssain!
Houssain Ali!
Ali How was Bisnager?
Houssain Fantastic! Landlord!

The Innkeeper enters briefly

Innkeeper Sir!
Houssain Make that two ales.
Innkeeper Right away, sir.

The Innkeeper goes

Houssain No, Bisnager was beautiful. A library such as you've never seen.
  Book upon book upon book. I spent the whole six months reading. Never
  moved.
Ali (*incredulously*) Really? And what about your gift? For the Princess?
  Have you brought her something from beyond her wildest dreams?
Houssain Of course, on my last day there. (*He indicates the carpet*) I bought
  it from this merchant. He must have thought it was his birthday.
Ali What is it?
Houssain What else? A magic carpet, of course.
Ali A magic carpet? Does it work?
Houssain Sssh! No, of course it doesn't. At least I sincerely hope not.
  Wouldn't do to bring her back something useful, would it? (*He laughs*)
  And you? What have you brought from Persia?
Ali Ah, Persia. Oh, the women in Persia, such women. You have no idea,
  Houssain...
Houssain And I don't want to know, thank you. Tell me, what have you
  brought her? Is that a telescope?
Ali Do you mind? A magic telescope, please. Through which you can see
  all that you wish to see. In any direction for a thousand miles.
Houssain Really?
Ali No, you can't see a blessed thing. You can't even see your hand through
  it. I think it's broken. But it cost me a fortune. A totally useless gift, eh?
Houssain Well, possibly. I still think my carpet takes a bit of beating. (*He
  realizes the joke*) Takes a bit of beating. (*He laughs*) Did you get that?
Ali (*dryly*) Yes...

Ahmed enters

Ahmed Houssain!

Houssain Ahmed!
Ahmed Ali!
Ali Ahmed!
Ahmed How are you both?
Houssain Never better. (*He calls*) Landlord!

The Innkeeper enters briefly

Innkeeper Sir?
Houssain Make that three ales.
Innkeeper Right away, sir.

The Innkeeper goes

Ali Now, Ahmed, what fantastic gift have you managed to purchase for our Princess? Can it beat my sightless telescope?
Houssain Or my non-flying carpet?
Ali What have you brought? Have you brought anything at all?
Houssain If not, that's cheating.
Ahmed No, I've brought something. Never fear. From the magical, wondrous land of Samarkand. (*He takes an apple from his pocket*) See here.
Ali What's that?
Ahmed What does it look like?
Houssain It looks like an ordinary apple.
Ahmed No. There you're wrong. This is no ordinary apple. This apple, dear brothers, is enchanted. One bite and all ills, all ailments are cured. This is the perfect medicine for all diseases.
Ali Really?
Ahmed No, not really. All it'll give you is indigestion. It's about the only thing in Samarkand that is guaranteed non-magical. Impressive, yes? Isn't this the worst possible gift? A sour, ordinary, common or garden apple?
Houssain (*a bit dismayed*) Yes.
Ali (*likewise*) Yes.
Ahmed It seems I may have won.
Houssain Possibly. But remember. There's hope for us, yet. Only one of us has to marry her.
Ali Yes. Let's look on the bright side.

The Innkeeper hurries through to the front door

Houssain Landlord, where's that ale?
Innkeeper A million pardons, sir. There's a magnificent coach outside. With a beautiful woman in it.

Ali Is my hair all right?
Innkeeper We very rarely get any magnificent coaches calling here, sir.
Ali What about beautiful women?
Innkeeper Oh, never, sir! Excuse me, please!

The Innkeeper goes out

Houssain Now, while we're alone, remember. Until the Princess has chosen
or not chosen, we must continue with the deception, telling no-one. We
must convince everybody we've done our best to win her. Even though
we've done our best to lose her. (*He extends his hand*) May the worst gifts
lose, brothers!
All (*joining hands*) May the worst gifts lose!

*The Innkeeper enters with an elegantly dressed woman. It is a transformed
Murganah*

The brothers gawk at her

Ali (*recovering first and bowing*) My lady!
Houssain (*bowing*) Madam!
Ahmed (*in amazement*) Murganah!
Houssain (*looking up*) Murganah?
Ali (*looking up*) Murganah?
Murganah My Lords! (*She curtsies*)
Houssain Landlord! Four ales!
Innkeeper Right away, sir! Just changing the barrel.

The Innkeeper goes

Ali What's happened to you, Murganah? You've changed so much in six
months.
Murganah I came in to a little—good fortune.
Houssain A large fortune by the look of it.
Ahmed You look—beautiful.
Murganah Thank you, Ahmed.
Houssain And how is the Princess?
Murganah Perfectly fit when I left her. And how have you all fared on your
travels? Have you brought back priceless gifts for the Princess?
Houssain (*with a look at the others*) Oh, famously. We have some unique
and spectacular gifts for her. A magic carpet.
Ali A magic telescope.
Murganah And what about you, Ahmed?

Ahmed (*sheepishly*) A magic apple.

Murganah An apple? You hope to win her with an apple?

Ahmed (*with a look at the others*) Yes. It's been done before.

Murganah (*coolly*) I see. May I look at the gifts? How does this telescope work?

Ali Ah, well, you merely have to imagine and you are able to see whatever you wish to see within a thousand miles radius. Apparently.

Murganah How wonderful! How does it work?

Ali (*looking through it*) Well, actually, it's not quite in working order yet, it's...

Murganah makes a gesture

Ah!

Houssain What is it?

Ali I can see through it. I can see her.

Ahmed See who?

Ali The Princess Nouronnihar. I just thought of her and I can see her. It's amazing. I was certain it wouldn't work... It's incredible.

Houssain (*taking it from him*) Let me look.

Ali Can you see her?

Houssain Yes. It's Nouronnihar.

Ahmed What is she doing?

Houssain She's lying deathly still. There are people round her bed. She's ill.

Ahmed Ill? (*He takes the telescope from him*) Yes, I see her. She's not ill. She seems to be dying.

Ali Dying!

Murganah Poor thing!

Houssain Dying!

Ali (*taking back the telescope*) We can't let her die. Not after all she's——

Houssain (*cutting him off*) We must go to her at once. Before it's too late.

Ahmed The Palace is a day's ride from here. We may be too late.

Murganah Why not use your carpet?

Houssain My what?

Murganah Your magic carpet? That should get you there in time.

Houssain Ah, yes. Well, the carpet, yes. It has—one or two teething problems. It's not very reliable. Just at present.

Murganah May I see?

Houssain Yes, of course. By all means.

The brothers unroll the carpet

As you see, it's a perfectly ordinary-looking rug but it does have these amazing powers. When they work.

Murganah So what do you have to do?
Houssain Well, we're all supposed to sit on it.
Murganah Sit on it? How?
Houssain (*sheepishly*) Like this.
Murganah All of you?
Houssain Yes. Come on, you two.

The other two join him

Ali (*softly to Houssain*) It's not going to start flying, is it?
Houssain (*softly*) Of course it isn't.
Murganah Now what happens?
Houssain Well, apparently all you have to do is say, "Carpet! Magic Carpet!
Take me to the Sultan's Palace"! And then it...

Murganah makes a gesture

Oh, good grief!

The carpet is suddenly lifting off the ground with the three brothers on it

Ali Oh, no...
Ahmed Whey-hey!
Houssain We're flying! It works! (*Dismayed*) It's not supposed to work!
Murganah Goodbye! See you at the Palace!

The Innkeeper enters with four glasses of ale on a tray

Innkeeper Sorry to keep you—four ales... What the...?
Murganah Goodbye!
Houssain Goodbye!
Ali Goodbye!
Ahmed Goodbye!
Innkeeper Who's paying for these ales? Come back!

*The Innkeeper and Murganah fade from sight as the brothers start their
flying journey*

Ahmed This is amazing!
Ali I can't look down. I can't stand heights!
Ahmed Look, there's the forest!
Houssain Why did it suddenly work?
Ahmed And the river.

Ali Tell me when it's over!
Ahmed Wheeeee!
Houssain There's the Palace, look!
Ali Thank heaven!
Ahmed So fast! This is the way to travel!
Houssain Look out, everyone, we're coming down!
Ali We're going to crash!
Ahmed No, we're not. Don't be so...
Houssain Brace yourselves!

The carpet lands and we are at:

SCENE 6

Nouronnihar's Bedside

The Sultan, Salim, the Vizier and Safia are standing around the bedside

The three Princes arrive

Vizier Good gracious!

Salim momentarily draws his sword to protect his Princess

Sultan Houssain! Ali! Ahmed! What is the meaning of this?
Houssain I'm sorry, Father, we heard the Princess was ill. We——
Sultan She is not ill, Houssain. The Princess is dying. I think you might have
    shown a little more consideration rather than bursting in like hooligans...
    How did you get in here, anyway?
Houssain We—we...
Ahmed ...had a lift...
Vizier A lift?
Ali Father, what has caused this illness? We met Murganah and she told us
    the Princess was perfectly fit a day or two ago...
Vizier (*worriedly*) Ah, yes. Murganah.
Sultan No. She's right. This illness suddenly struck the Princess, soon after
    Murganah left to meet you. The doctors say there is nothing—nothing that
    can save her, poor girl. Now please leave and show some respect.
Houssain (*softly, to the others*) What are we going to do?
Ali Well, at least we don't have to marry her.
Ahmed Don't say that. We can't just let her die.
Ali What can we do?

Houssain What about the apple?
Ahmed The apple?
Houssain Your apple...
Ahmed (*to Houssain*) That's no good. It's just an ordinary apple.
Houssain The other things worked.
Ali Mine was just an ordinary broken telescope...
Houssain Mine was just a useless old carpet...
Ali Go on!
Houssain Why not?

Ahmed moves towards the bed

Ahmed Er ... Father...
Sultan What is it? Are you still here, boy?
Ahmed (*tentatively*) I have something that may help the Princess...
Sultan Help? What is it?
Ahmed It's a—it's a—magic apple...
Sultan A magic apple?
Vizier Did he say a magic apple? I thought he said a magic apple...
Ahmed Here! (*He shows the apple*)
Sultan Don't be so ridiculous...
Houssain Please let him try it, Father.
Ali It could work.
Sultan What, an apple?
Ahmed It's a magic apple.
Houssain Please!
Ali Please!
Ahmed It's worth a try.
Salim Try.
Sultan (*reluctantly*) I warn you, I shall be very angry indeed if this is some
    sort of joke.
Ahmed (*approaching Nouronnihar*) It's not a joke, Father. I promise you.

*Ahmed, assisted by Safia, props up the Princess's head and persuades her to
nibble the apple. Nouronnihar coughs and splutters and spits it out*

    (*Distraught*) It doesn't work.
Sultan Just as I suspected. Ahmed! You will come to my chambers in five
    minutes. I'm going to have you flogged and thrown in a dungeon, young
    man. And as for you two—bread and water for ten weeks.
Ali Ten weeks!
Houssain Father! What have we done?
Sultan (*as he goes*) For encouraging him. Five minutes, Ahmed!

Salim Fool!

The Sultan sweeps out with Salim

Vizier (*as he follows*) Appalling behaviour. You should be ashamed of yourselves, all of you.

Vizier goes out

Houssain Well, thank you very much.
Ali Bread and water for ten weeks. What will that do to my figure?
Ahmed Well, at least it didn't work...
Houssain Obviously it didn't work. You idiot!
Ali You fool...

Ali and Houssain go out

Ahmed (*vainly after them*) But it was never supposed to— (*he is alone*) — work. (*He moves back to the bedside. To the unconscious Nouronnihar*) I'm sorry. If I could do anything, I would, Princess.

Murganah appears in the shadows

Murganah There's nothing.
Ahmed (*startled*) Murganah... How did you get here?
Murganah I have some very fast transport of my own. There's nothing you can do for her, Ahmed. She's dying. Your pretty little Princess is dying.
Ahmed She can't die. She's so young. I mean, I——
Murganah Love her?
Ahmed No. Yes.
Murganah You do?
Ahmed Yes.
Murganah Then you'd better kiss her goodbye.
Ahmed Murganah, if there's any way you can help... I mean, I saw you with the telescope and the carpet... I don't know how you did it but... Can't you do the same with this apple? Make it work as it's supposed to work?
Murganah What if I could?
Ahmed Please.
Murganah Why should I? Why should I save her life?
Ahmed Because we can't just let her die. We can't. Please, Murganah. If you love me at all...
Murganah Oh, love, love, love...
Ahmed All right, not love. Common humanity. Murganah. I beg you.

Murganah (*after a fractional hesitation*) Try it again. Try your apple again.
Ahmed Thank you. (*He tries the apple on the Princess as before*)

Safia assists. Murganah gestures. This time the Princess slowly revives

Nouronnihar (*drowsily*) Whar ... whar ... what ... what ... what happ—
where?
Ahmed It's all right, I'm here. It's all right.
Nouronnihar You? You're back? I've had such terrible dreams. Frightening
dreams. He was coming for me...
Ahmed Coming for you? Who was coming for you?
Nouronnihar The man—the dead man in the cloak...
Murganah (*startled*) Who?
Ahmed What is she saying?
Murganah Nothing. She's delirious...
Ahmed She's cured. (*He calls*) The Princess is cured. Come quickly, the
Princess is cured!

Houssain, Ali, the Sultan, and the Vizier enter

Houssain		Cured?
Ali		You mean it worked?
Sultan	(*together*)	What is the meaning of this? What's happened?
Vizier		Cured? She's cured? It's a miracle.
Salim		It has worked?

Nouronnihar Ahmed! You cured me?
Ahmed In a way, yes...
Nouronnihar Then you are the one I must marry.
Salim He is the one she must marry!
All (*except Ahmed*) Hooray!
Ahmed Ah, yes... But if we had not got here so swiftly on Houssain's magic
carpet we would have been too late to save you...
Nouronnihar Then maybe it is Houssain I should marry.
Salim He is the one she must marry!
All (*except Houssain*) Hooray!
Houssain Ah, no, but if we had not looked through Ali's telescope, we would
never have known you were ill. It was all entirely due to Ali...
Nouronnihar Then perhaps it is Ali I should marry...
Salim He is the one she must marry!
All (*except Ali*) Hooray!
Nouronnihar I don't know. I'm confused. Someone help me decide.
Sultan It appears we need another competition.
Houssain Oh, good.

Ali Another one?

Ahmed Where are we going this time?

Vizier Might I suggest, sire...

Sultan Grand Vizier?

Vizier Might I suggest—that rather than another quest, a test. The test of the arrows.

Sultan Of course! The test of the arrows! What a brilliant idea of mine! So be it. Follow me. And after this test is over, tell the kitchens to prepare a feast for two hundred.

The Sultan, the Vizier, Nouronnihar, Salim and Safia leave

The brothers start to follow them

Ahmed What's the test of the arrows?

Ali Search me.

Houssain Haven't the faintest idea.

Sultan (*off*) Follow me, boys!

Ali Follow him!

Ali and Houssain leave

Ahmed is about to follow. Murganah, unnoticed in the corner, calls him back

Murganah (*softly*) Ahmed...

Ahmed Murganah, I... Thank you.

Murganah (*amused*) For saving you from a flogging? From keeping you from the dungeon?

Ahmed You know what I mean.

Murganah I promised I'd always look after you... Now's your chance to do something for me.

Ahmed How do you mean?

Murganah It's the test of the arrows. Each of you must fire an arrow up into the Mountain of Storms. He who manages to fire his arrow farthest wins. You have only to fire short of your brothers and one of them must marry her. And then you'll be mine. Mine, Ahmed. As it was meant to be. And I shall be yours.

Ahmed (*uncertainly*) Yes...

Murganah See how beautiful I have become for you, Ahmed. I did this for you. Don't you think I'm more beautiful than her? Than your little idiot Princess. Don't you?

Ahmed Yes.

Murganah Then lose for me. I can make you rich, I can give you power, I

can make you happy... Anyone who stands in our way, we can crush them.
We can destroy them...

Ahmed Murganah... What's happened to you? You've changed so much.
You've grown colder...

Murganah I've grown up, that's all. I've realized that in this life, what you
want you take. You don't wait, you don't ask. You take. The world is made
up of givers and takers. I am a winner and I take all. Join with me, Ahmed,
and we'll win together. But first of all, you must lose this contest. Come
on.

Murganah goes out

Ahmed (*as he follows her, worriedly*) Oh, Murganah...

As Ahmed goes, the scene changes

SCENE 7

At the foot of The Mountain of Storms

*Everyone is assembling. The Sultan, the Vizier, Salim, Nouronnihar with
Safia, Houssain, Ali and finally Murganah and Ahmed*

Sultan Very well. If we are all assembled, let the contest begin. My eldest
son will fire first. Give the bow to Houssain.

The Vizier hands the long bow to Houssain

Ali (*softly, to Houssain*) I bet I can shoot less far than you can.

Houssain Want to bet. Watch this. (*He draws back the bow and fires the
arrow*)

*Murganah gestures. The others watch the arrow's flight, shading their eyes
and ooohing and aaahing*

Vizier Heavens! It's gone for miles.

Sultan Good shot, Houssain! Didn't know you had it in you, my boy.

Ali (*amused*) Good shot!

Houssain I must have—I must have misfired.

Ahmed (*to Murganah*) How did Houssain shoot that far? He normally
hasn't the strength to lift up a bow.

Murganah It's a mystery to me. (*She smiles*)

Salim He is the one she must marry!
Sultan Not yet, not yet, Salim! Ali, my second son. See if you can match
   Houssain's fine shot.
Ali I'll do my best not to—not to let you down, Father!
Sultan Good boy!

The Vizier hands the bow to Ali who prepares to shoot

Ali Watch this, Houssain… (*He shoots*)

Murganah gestures. The others watch, shading their eyes, and ooh and ahhh

Vizier It's cleared the trees.
Sultan It's even better.
Ali Oh, no!
Vizier Amazing!
Sultan Brilliant shooting, lad!
Ahmed Oh, Murganah!
Ali Come back! Come back! You stupid arrow!
Houssain (*applauding sarcastically*) Well done!
Salim He is the one she must marry!
Sultan Not yet, not yet, Salim. So far, Ali is the winner. But come along,
   young Ahmed. Let's see what you can do.
Ahmed I'll try, Father. I don't think I'll be able to beat my brothers.
Murganah I doubt it.
Sultan Never lose heart, boy. You can do it.

Ahmed is handed the bow. He prepares to shoot

Ahmed Right. Here I go. (*He shoots*)

A disappointed noise from the crowd

Sultan Oh, come on, boy. That hasn't gone more than two… Good heavens.
   What's happening? Just look at that! I thought it had landed.
Vizier It must be the wind. A freak gust of wind. There it goes.

*Everyone shades their eyes following the arrow. It goes higher and higher
up the mountain. Much ooohing and aaahing*

Houssain Good shot!
Ali Well done!
Ahmed (*to Murganah*) Did I do that?

Murganah (*frowning*) No...
Ahmed Did you do that?
Murganah No. But somebody did.
Nouronnihar Bravo! (*She bounds up to Ahmed*) The winner!
Salim He is the one she must marry!
Sultan Ah, no, no, Princess. Don't be too impatient. There is still the second half of the trial for them to complete. Grand Vizier!
Vizier Each contestant must now climb the mountain and further prove their prowess by retrieving his own arrow and presenting it to the Princess. May the best man win. It looks like you have quite a climb ahead of you, young Ahmed. No-one has ever climbed that high on the Mountain of Storms.
Ahmed Oh, great.
Houssain Good luck, Ahmed. I'll be back for tea.
Ali Should make it home by supper time.
Houssain See you, brother. Good shooting.
Ali (*clapping Ahmed on the shoulder*) Didn't know you had it in you. 'Bye.

Houssain and Ali go off up the mountain

Sultan You can see for yourself, Salim, what fine sons I've bred, eh?
Salim He is the one she must marry!
Sultan Yes, yes. All in good time, Salim. (*To the Vizier*) I think he may have gone wrong again, don't you?
Vizier I will have our workshops look at him again, sire. But they do tell me that rust has taken its toll.
Sultan Ah me! Well, it happens to us all. Come along.
Vizier I think we may need to postpone the feast, sire, till they return.
Sultan Oh, really? I suppose we must. That's a pity...

The Sultan and the Vizier go off with Salim

Ahmed Well, here I go.
Nouronnihar (*kissing him*) Good luck. I'll be waiting.
Ahmed Thank you. (*To Murganah*) See you soon.

Murganah does not reply

Yes. Right.

Ahmed goes off

Nouronnihar (*seeing Murganah*) Murganah? I hardly recognized you. If I've told you once, I've told you a hundred times, why are you still unveiled in my presence?

Murganah (*looking at her dangerously*) I'm sorry, Princess. (*She pulls up her veil*)

Nouronnihar Once more, I'll have you punished. As I had to do with Safia there. Have you noticed how little she talks? There's a reason for that. She'd tell you if she could. (*She brightens*) Do you know, assuming I have to marry one of them, which of course I have to sooner or later—I'm glad it's Ahmed. Assuming he gets down safely off that wretched mountain. I do think he's the sweetest of the three of them. I really do. Yes, I've made a good choice. Come along. It's getting cold. Yes, an excellent choice.

Nouronnihar goes out, followed by Safia

Murganah (*as she goes, to herself*) It could be your last choice as well. (*With one last glance up the mountain*) Bring him down safely ... bring him back to me and only me...

Murganah leaves as the scene changes abruptly

SCENE 8

Near the summit of The Mountain of Storms

A bleak mountainside not far from the summit. The wind is getting up

Ahmed appears. He is breathless from his climb. He pauses for a brief rest

Ahmed How much higher? Where is it? Where are you, arrow? I couldn't have shot it this far. Nobody in the world could shoot an arrow to this height.

The wind increases

It's getting difficult to see. The mist's getting thicker... Just a bit higher. Nearly at the top... (*He climbs a bit further*)

The wind increases to a howl. Suddenly Ahmed is in the midst of a blizzard. He is whirled this way and that

Help... I can't stand up. Help! Help me! (*He starts to slip and slide, finally falling to his knees*)

The blizzard continues to rage

Suddenly out of the snow storm and the darkness emerges a rather frightening-looking figure, totally muffled against the cold. Huge and rather menacing, a cross between a Yeti and an Egyptian mummy. The figure approaches Ahmed

(*Alarmed*) What the...? Who are...? Who are...? Ah... (*He faints clean away*)

As Ahmed starts to fall, the figure catches him and effortlessly lifts the inert body. As it carries Ahmed away into the blizzard the Lights fade to Black-out

ACT II

SCENE 1

Paribanou's Mountain Palace

Her palace is a vast cave, lit by torch light. Jewelled and glittering, beautiful but eerily empty. It is inhabited only by Paribanou and Nasuh, her servant

Nasuh enters. Although he has removed his bulky outer protective clothing which made him appear even more giant-like, he remains a large powerful figure. He carries the inert body of Ahmed

In the shadows, almost indiscernible at this point, Paribanou appears

Paribanou (*from the shadows*) How is he?
Nasuh Still unconscious.
Paribanou Take him to the chamber.

Nasuh starts to do so

   Do you think he will prove worthy?
Nasuh Who knows? He weighs less than a feather. I wouldn't care to stake my life on him.
Paribanou I think we may both have to, Nasuh. He could well be our last chance. Come, bring him.

   Paribanou leads the way as Nasuh carries Ahmed off. As this happens, the scene changes

SCENE 2

The Sultan's Palace

The Sultan enters. From another direction, simultaneously, the Grand Vizier also hurries on with Salim following

Sultan Still no sign?

Vizier Sire, it has been two days now. Two days and two freezing nights. I fear no-one could have survived on that mountain.

Sultan Then Ahmed is dead?

Vizier I fear so, sire. We have had search parties combing the hills. He must have climbed higher than the snow line.

Sultan But how could an arrow fired by an ordinary bow come to soar so high? It's inexplicable.

Vizier A freak wind, sire. That's all we can assume.

Salim If the boy is dead, then his brother must be declared the winner.

Sultan Oh, good, they got him working again. Yes, Salim, you are right. If Ahmed has perished, then it is Ali who must marry the Princess Nouronnihar. We will break the news to them. Send them here, Grand Vizier.

Vizier My Lord, they are waiting outside for news.

Sultan Bring them.

The Vizier goes to the door and calls softly

Vizier Please ... will you all come in.

Houssain, Ali, Nouronnihar and Murganah enter

Sultan I have sad news of Ahmed. I fear he has been lost on the mountain. We must assume him dead.

Ali turns to Houssain and they clasp each other for a moment in grief. Nouronnihar clasps a hand to her mouth and gives a stifled cry. Only Murganah appears unmoved

It would seem, under such sad circumstances, that Ali will receive the hand of Nouronnihar in marriage. There will be some appropriate days of mourning for Ahmed and the wedding will then be announced officially. God bless you both. God help us all.

Salim He is the one she must marry!

Sultan Oh, no. Not again!

The Sultan leaves, followed by the Vizier and Salim

A silence

Ali Well. Would that these were happier circumstances to announce an engagement. (*To Nouronnihar*) I hope—I will try to be a good husband, Nouronnihar.

Nouronnihar Thank you. (*As she goes, tearfully*) I'm delighted to hear it.

Nouronnihar goes out, weeping

Ali What will you do, brother?
Houssain Me? What I always knew I would do. I shall become a hermit. I
shall shut myself away somewhere in a remote place, far from civilisation
and I shall study my books. Try to unravel the mysteries of this world. Like
why people as good and true as Ahmed should die so needlessly. (*He starts
to leave*)
Ali Won't you even stay for the wedding?
Houssain (*distressed*) I couldn't, Ali, I'm sorry. I must go straightaway. I'm
sorry. I wish you every happiness, brother. Goodbye.

Houssain goes

Ali Goodbye, Houssain. (*Half to himself*) It seems I have lost two brothers
in a single day. And what have I gained? A wife whom I suspect doesn't
want me. What a bargain!
Murganah Nouronnihar will grow to love you. Never fear.
Ali You think so?
Murganah Give her time. And patience. Tenderness and encouragement.
Ali Encouragement?
Murganah Give her loving gifts. (*She produces a small ornamental jar*)
Like this.
Ali What is it?
Murganah Oranges. Preserved in rare spices. Spices with magical properties.
Encourage her to eat one slice a day. I promise she will hour by hour grow
more beautiful, more loving…
Ali Can that be so?
Murganah Take them as a wedding gift. I was saving them for my own
wedding day but now… (*She breaks off, apparently overcome*)
Ali Thank you, Murganah. I am very touched. (*He takes the jar from her*)
Thank you. (*He moves away*)
Murganah (*as he goes*) One a day, mind. And watch the difference in her.

Ali goes

(*Smiling to herself*) Just watch her grow.

As Murganah leaves, the scene changes

SCENE 3

Paribanou's Mountain Palace

Ahmed is standing

Nasuh enters

Nasuh Are you feeling stronger?
Ahmed A little, thank you. That was an excellent breakfast. My compliments to your cook, whoever it is.
Nasuh Me.
Ahmed Ah. Well, thank you. But would you please tell me where I am and who you are? What is this place? It's like a cave, only—only as if it's made of rare jewels.
Nasuh It is the nature of the rock. It stores and reflects light. Light from many millions of years ago when the sun was so bright it saw fit to shine here.

Paribanou enters unobserved

Ahmed And you? How did you come to be here? More important, how did I come to be here?
Paribanou You must ask your questions of me, not Nasuh. (*She steps forward for the first time into the light*) Welcome, Ahmed.
Ahmed (*impressed*) Madam, I—I have not—I have not had the pleasure.
Paribanou My name is Paribanou.
Ahmed A princess?
Paribanou (*smiling*) No. Not a princess.
Ahmed Then who...? How did you know my name? How did I...?
Paribanou Leave us, please, Nasuh.
Nasuh Mistress. (*He bows*)

Nasuh exits

Paribanou (*gently*) Sit down. We have much to talk about. But first I must explain a little. You are owed that. Do you like fairy tales, Ahmed?
Ahmed (*laughing*) Well. It depends. I used to.
Paribanou Listen to this one. And pay attention. Once upon a time there were two children. A sister and a brother. Their mother had died when they were very young and as a result the brother's behaviour was often very wild. They were brought up by their father, a good and powerful wizard in the most happy of kingdoms. One day it happened that the father had to leave them in order to make a journey. He left them in the care of the

servants and before he went he bade them to be good and well behaved during his absence. If they were good, he said, when he returned he would reward them with wonderful gifts. And it happened that whilst he was away, although the daughter obeyed her father, the brother did not. Instead he meddled with his father's spell books, and not only tormented his sister but was cruel to the servants. In fact, he became so wild and uncontrollable that when the father returned, the palace was all but in ruins. For by then the son, in his search for wealth and power, had sold his very soul to Schaibar himself...

Ahmed Schaibar?

Paribanou Schaibar, the Stranger from the Darkness who seeks to lead us all into that same Darkness. Anyway, the wizard could do nothing, realizing he had lost his only son for ever. And he became first sad and then angry with his daughter for just feebly standing by and doing nothing to stop her brother. And her punishment was to remain in a beautiful but lonely cave high on a mountain. A prison she could never leave until she learnt to stand up for what is right and to oppose all that is bad. And here she has remained to this day. Alone with only Nasuh for company. You are the first visitor this place has ever seen, Ahmed. Welcome.

Ahmed Why me?

Paribanou Maybe you were sent? Who knows?

Ahmed And your brother? What became of him?

Paribanou Alas, he has long ago gone to the Darkness. But there are others since who have made bargains with Schaibar. Others who seek to rule the world through uncertainty and fear.

Ahmed But how can you do anything if you're unable to leave this place?

Paribanou If I am ever to be free, then I need a Champion.

Ahmed A Champion?

Paribanou One such as you, Ahmed.

Ahmed Me? I'm no Champion, I'm afraid. I can't fight, I can't run, I can't climb. I'm not very brave and I'm frightened of spiders.

Paribanou You can shoot arrows, though.

Ahmed Yes. Yes, that's true. I can shoot arrows. But not much else, I'm afraid.

Paribanou You will learn. Nasuh will teach you.

Ahmed I really think he'd be wasting his time.

Paribanou Please, Ahmed. You're surely my last hope. Won't you consider it?

Ahmed It's just that there are dozens of others better qualified than I.

Paribanou There is only you. You've been sent. Please.

Ahmed (*considering*) I owe you my life. I acknowledge that. I suppose the least I can do is... You couldn't have found a worse man. That's all I'm saying. You're probably stronger than I am.

Paribanou Physical strength is not everything. There is a strength that lies within you, too. Is it a bargain?

Ahmed I am—yours to command... (*He extends his hand*) Paribanou...

Paribanou (*taking his hand*) Come with me, my Champion, there is no time to lose.

They start to leave

Ahmed I hope you know what you're doing.

As Ahmed and Paribanou leave, the scene changes

SCENE 4

The Sultan's Palace

Wedding bells

Nouronnihar comes on in her wedding dress which appears a trifle tight on her. Murganah fusses round her

Nouronnihar (*in a frenzy*) ...No, no, no. That's not right. You're not going to make it right doing that, are you, you stupid girl?

Murganah (*patiently*) Princess, please hold still. (*She tries to adjust the dress*)

Nouronnihar This ridiculous dress. That stupid dressmaker. How could she make it two sizes too small? I mean look at it! I look absurd. I can't appear like this on my wedding day. People are simply going to laugh.

Murganah Princess, it hardly notices... It really doesn't!

Nouronnihar When I get hold of that dressmaker I'll have her head cut off. That'll teach her!

Murganah Princess, that would hardly be fair. You may have put on a tiny, tiny little bit of weight...

Nouronnihar Weight? Me? Put on weight? How dare you say that? Right, that's your tongue cut out!

Murganah (*unconcerned*) Yes, Princess.

Nouronnihar And your head as well.

Murganah Yes, Princess. There, that looks much better.

Nouronnihar (*anxiously*) Is it better? Does it look better?

Murganah You look ravishing.

Nouronnihar I'm so nervous. Why am I so nervous? An orange slice. Give me another orange slice.

Murganah Are you sure, Princess? You've had three slices this morning
already.

Nouronnihar (*loudly*) I need a slice of orange. Give me one or I'll have your
feet cut off as well.

Murganah Certainly, Princess. (*She produces the ornamental jar and opens
it*)

Nouronnihar takes a slice of orange and gobbles it greedily

The Sultan enters with Salim

Sultan Where is she? Where is the bride? They're all waiting! Everyone's
sitting there waiting!

Murganah She's ready, sire, she's ready now.

Sultan What is she doing? For heaven's sake, is the girl eating?

Murganah The happy bride is ready.

Sultan (*to Nouronnihar*) About time, too. Come, Salim, give the Princess
your arm.

Salim removes one of his arms and offers it to Nouronnihar

Salim Here.

Nouronnihar squawks and recoils in horror

Sultan Oh, dear heavens, the man is impossible these days. (*He proffers his
own arm*) Here, Princess. Have one of mine.

Nouronnihar Thank you. (*She extends her arm*)

There is a ripping sound as her dress gives

Oh, no! What was that?

Murganah Nothing, Princess...

Nouronnihar (*hysterically*) It's split! My dress has split! My dress has split!

Murganah Keep calm! It's a tiny tear, Princess. No-one will notice if you
don't lift your arms. Now keep calm. That's better.

Nouronnihar calms down

Sultan Thank you, Murganah! Someone at least with a modicum of sense.
(*To Nouronnihar*) Now come along! And pull yourself together, girl.

The Sultan practically drags Nouronnihar off

Salim follows, still holding his arm

Salim He is the man she must marry!

Salim exits

Murganah smiles to herself and follows them off. As she does so, the scene changes

SCENE 5

Paribanou's Mountain Palace

Ahmed and Nasuh are preparing to fight. Paribanou watches them

Nasuh (*shaping up to fight*) All right. Once more. Come at me again, but this time keeping your guard.

Ahmed hesitates uncertainly

Come on, attack me! Lunge, lunge!

Finally, Ahmed makes a clumsy dash at Nasuh who easily evades the charge and helps Ahmed on his way with a kick in the pants

Ahmed sails past Nasuh and disappears off. A crash and a yell as he collides with something

Ahmed (*off*) Aaaahh!

Nasuh looks at Paribanou and shrugs

Paribanou (*concerned*) Oh dear...

As Nasuh and Paribanou go off after Ahmed, the scene changes

SCENE 6

The Sultan's Palace

The wedding feast. Music

The Sultan, the Vizier, Salim, Nouronnihar, Ali and Murganah are present

Murganah approaches the Sultan with a goblet of wine

Murganah More wine, sire.
Sultan Ah! Should I now? I've had several glasses already. The sooner we
sit down to that feast, the better. Oh, it's a wedding after all. Why not?
Thank you, Murganah.
Murganah It is my honour to serve you, sire.
Sultan Good, good. No, don't run away. You've grown increasingly mature,
Murganah, over these last few months. I'm impressed with your progress.
I have to say that in the past, your conduct sometimes left a lot to be desired.
Running around the place like a savage.
Murganah I hope I have learned better, sire.
Sultan You've—er... You've also grown very beautiful.
Murganah (*humbly*) Thank you, sire. You, of course, remember the ancient
proverb. A woman is made more beautiful when she stands in the shadow
of a handsome man.
Sultan (*embarrassed*) Ha! Yes. Very good. I like that. Never heard it before.
Thank you very much. I'll remember that. Handsome man, yes. (*He laughs
some more*)

Murganah moves away, laughing too. The Vizier moves to her angrily

Vizier Murganah! (*He draws her to one side*) What on earth are you playing
at, girl?
Murganah (*puzzled*) I'm sorry, Father.
Vizier Do you realize what you are doing? Publicly disporting yourself like
that? A mere servant, flirting with the Sultan himself! How dare you? I am
speechless at your behaviour, Murganah! Absolutely! I would like——

Murganah places her fingers on her father's mouth

Murganah And speechless you will remain, Father. You will never speak
to me like that again. (*She moves away swiftly*)

The Vizier touches his mouth, startled. The music stops. A fanfare

Sultan I shall now call upon the Grand Vizier to ask our young couple to commence the dancing. Grand Vizier!

The Vizier appears to find it impossible to open his mouth. He makes muffled sounds

Grand Vizier!

More muffled sounds from the Vizier

How extraordinary! What on earth's the matter, man?
Murganah Maybe he's eaten some toffee.
Sultan (*finding this very funny*) Toffee! Yes, very funny. Ah well. I'll do it myself. I call upon our beautiful young couple to lead the dancing!
Salim (*in a grand voice*) Highness His Ali Prince and Royal Her Princess Highness Nouronnihar—har—har—har—har——
Sultan Oh, do stop it! (*He hits Salim*)

A piece falls off Salim. Ali and Nouronnihar step forward together. As the music starts up they begin to dance. Everyone claps. The dancers twirl. Suddenly Nouronnihar's dress splits completely

Nouronnihar screams and runs from the floor

The music stops

Ali (*hurrying after her*) Nouronnihar!

Ali exits

Sultan (*recovering the situation*) All right! That's quite enough dancing! Time for the feast! Bring on the feast!
Murganah I think under the circumstances, sire, that it might be— inappropriate.
Sultan How do you mean?
Murganah The Princess seems rather distressed. Perhaps it would be tactless to continue with the celebrations.
Sultan You think so? I suppose you're right. That's a pity. Cancel the feast then. (*He calls as he goes*) Cancel the feast!

The Sultan has gone off. The others follow him, the Vizier making more muffled sounds. As they do so, the scene changes

SCENE 7

Paribanou's Mountain Palace

Ahmed and Nasuh are still practising

Ahmed enters with his sword, moving backwards as if he has been given a giant shove by Nasuh

Ahmed Aaaaaahhh! (*He sits with a bump*)

Nasuh enters, holding a sword

Nasuh How many times do I have to tell you?
Ahmed I'll never learn.
Nasuh (*fiercely*) You must learn!
Ahmed (*angrily*) I can't. I give up! All right? I take back what I said. I'm nobody's Champion. I couldn't possibly be. If this was a real fight I'd have been dead twenty times over. What is the point? I'm sorry, I give up. (*He throws down his sword*)

Paribanou appears in a doorway

Paribanou Ahmed!
Ahmed I want to go home. I want to see my father. I want to see my brothers.
Paribanou Soon.
Ahmed Now!
Paribanou Please.
Ahmed (*weakening*) I—I—need to see them.
Paribanou Please. For me. My Champion.
Ahmed Your Champion? That's a laugh. I don't even know what all this is about. What I'm even training for. Who I shall even be fighting.
Paribanou All will be revealed in time. I promise.
Ahmed When?
Paribanou When the time is right. When the agent of Schaibar finally reveals themself. (*She picks up his sword*) Please. For me.
Ahmed (*wearily*) For you. Yes. For you. (*He takes his sword from her and makes another lunge at Nasuh*) The Champion of Paribanoooooo…

Again he is booted offstage. Another crash

Nasuh looks at Paribanou and shrugs hopelessly

Nasuh (*as he goes*) Now, what did I tell you…?

Nasuh goes off after Ahmed

Paribanou (*as she goes, worriedly to herself*) Oh dear, oh dear...

Paribanou exits

SCENE 8

The Sultan's Palace Gardens

Nouronnihar, who has grown even larger than when we last saw her, is unhappily walking in the gardens

Murganah enters

Murganah Excuse me, Princess. Breakfast is served.

Nouronnihar I don't want any breakfast.

Murganah Princess, you must eat. You had no dinner yesterday and no lunch.

Nouronnihar I know that! I've had nothing to eat for days. I'm starving. Nothing but those wretched oranges. I should be as thin as a stick and look at me.

Murganah (*rather coyly*) Perhaps, Princess, we are expecting a happy event.

Nouronnihar (*angrily*) No, we are not expecting a happy event. There hasn't even been a happy event to make a happy event. My husband hasn't been near me for ages. (*Tearfully*) He can't stand the sight of me.

Murganah Oh, Princess, that's not true. His Highness worships the very——

Nouronnihar Is his Highness having breakfast with me?

Murganah I fear he's busy with affairs of state, Princess.

Nouronnihar Is he expected for lunch?

Murganah A meeting with the Household, Princess.

Nouronnihar Or tea?

Murganah He's inspecting the Guard, Princess.

Nouronnihar (*getting increasingly hysterical*) Or supper?

Murganah A state banquet.

Nouronnihar Or bed time?

Murganah I couldn't possibly say, Princess.

Nouronnihar There you are then. He's as good as left me after three weeks. What am I going to do?

Murganah Might I suggest, Princess, that a little of this... (*she produces a small jar of cream*) ...could do wonders.

Nouronnihar (*suspiciously*) What is it? I hope it works better than those oranges.

Murganah A special face cream, Princess. It's miraculous for the complexion. I swear by it myself. See. How smooth it is.

Nouronnihar Yes. You have—lovely skin... Probably born with it. You're very lucky.

Murganah I assure you it's due to this cream, Princess. A little rubbed in, night and morning, is all that's required.

Nouronnihar Yes? (*She takes the jar*) This had better work. If it doesn't I'll—I'll have your toes chopped off. One by one.

Murganah If it does not work, may I walk forever toeless, Princess.

Nouronnihar (*as she goes, looking back at her*) Yes. You do. You have lovely skin. Kindly put on your veil at once. How many more times?

Murganah (*curtsying*) Of course, Princess.

As Nouronnihar goes off, Murganah draws on her veil. As soon as Nouronnihar has gone, Ali creeps on

Ali (*furtively*) Murganah...

Murganah Your Highness...

Ali Has she gone? My wife?

Murganah The Princess has gone to her chambers, your Highness.

Ali Stop calling me that, for heaven's sake. It's Ali.

Murganah I am only a servant, your Highness. As the Princess is continually kind enough to remind me.

Ali Nonsense. You grew up with us. You're Murganah. You're a friend.

Murganah We all have our duty to perform, your Highness.

Ali Murganah, I need your help. You see. I don't think I love my wife. Isn't that terrible? I don't think I ever did. After all, you can't really hope to love a woman you've won in a competition. Well, I didn't even win, I came second. It's not unnatural of me not to love her, is it?

Murganah It's not uncommon, your Highness.

Ali No. Well, I feel terrible. I feel I've failed. It doesn't help that she seems to be— (*he indicates*) —you know. I mean, strictly between ourselves, we've taken to separate beds. We had to, there's no room for me in hers. What am I going to do? Help me, Murganah. Please... Do you despise me for saying this? Look, I wish you'd take off that stupid veil so I could see what you were thinking.

Murganah I have been commanded by the Princess to wear it, your Highness. I am forbidden to remove it.

Ali Well, she hasn't forbidden me. I'll remove it. (*He hesitates*) May I?

Murganah You are my Prince. I am yours to command.

Ali Yes. (*He removes her veil*) There. That's better. (*He stares at her*) You've grown even more beautiful, Murganah.

Murganah Thank you, your Highness.
Ali (*transfixed by her*) I—I—I could—if I wasn't—I could almost... I think
I'll go and have breakfast. And a cold bath. Take my mind off things. I'll
talk to you again.
Murganah (*curtsying*) Your Highness.

Ali hurries off

Murganah smiles to herself

The Vizier hurries across

Good morning, Father. Lovely day.

The Vizier makes a few muffled angry sounds and goes off

Murganah laughs and follows. As she does so, the scene changes

                                   Scene 9

Paribanou's Mountain Palace

Ahmed comes on slowly. He is listless and depressed. He sits

Paribanou comes on with Nasuh. They observe him anxiously

Paribanou (*to Nasuh, quietly*) What on earth's wrong with him?
Nasuh He's lost heart completely. He's been like this all day. There is no
fight left in him. I fear he will never become a Champion. It's as if his
strength was draining from him minute by minute.
Paribanou What can we do? He's our only hope. Oh, of all the men the gods
could have sent us... Is there nothing to be done with him?
Nasuh He—needs to see his family. To tell his father, his brothers that he's
alive. He misses them.
Paribanou He must love them very much.
Nasuh (*sadly*) It must be good to have a family.
Paribanou (*affectionately*) Oh, poor Nasuh... Then there's nothing for it.
He will have to return to his family, won't he?
Nasuh But how can he? Once he goes from here, he——
Paribanou Ahmed!
Ahmed (*feebly*) Hallo.
Paribanou I have an offer to make to you. If you will continue to practise
with Nasuh—prepare yourself to be my Champion...

Ahmed I can't. I'm sorry, I can't.

Paribanou Wait, let me finish! I will allow you return to your family for one hour.

Ahmed (*brightening*) You will?

Paribanou Is it a bargain?

Ahmed I may see my family again?

Paribanou For one hour only. And there are two conditions, Ahmed. You must tell no-one where you have been. If necessary, you must invent a story. Not a word about us. If the forces of Schaibar learn about our plan, you will be in grave danger. Do you promise?

Ahmed I promise.

Paribanou Secondly, you will also swear to return to us after an hour?

Ahmed I promise.

Paribanou Then prepare for the journey. We will find you some fresh clothes.

Ahmed (*as he goes*) I shall be ready to leave immediately...

Ahmed goes out

Nasuh What if he is followed on his return?

Paribanou No-one will be able to follow him, you know that. This Palace is invisible to all but him. And once he is close enough, he will become invisible as well.

Nasuh Not that he'll ever return.

Paribanou He'll return. He gave his word. His word as a Champion. Don't worry, Nasuh, he will return.

They go off. As they do so, the scene changes

SCENE 10

The Sultan's Palace Gardens. It is nearly dawn

Ali creeps on

Ali (*calling quietly*) Murganah! Murganah! Are you there?

Murganah steps from the shadows

Murganah Your Highness...

Ali moves to her and takes her hands

Ali Oh, Murganah. Thank heaven you got my message. I had to see you. I know it's wrong. I have a wife there in bed asleep. I know I should be faithful to her. But it's you I've always loved, Murganah. I swear it is.
Murganah What a shame you didn't show it at the time, your Highness...
Ali I'll make up for it now, Murganah, I promise. I'll take you away to a distant land where we'll——

A cry from Nouronnihar off

What was that?
Murganah It sounded like your wife, your Highness.

Another cry

Ali It is my wife. Quickly. (*He moves away from Murganah*)

Nouronnihar enters. Her face appears to have sprouted hair

Nouronnihar My face! Look at my face! What's happened to my face? Ali...
Ali (*looking at her in horror*) Oh! Oh! Aaaaaah!

Ali rushes out in horror

Nouronnihar What am I going to do? Look at me, Murganah. What am I going to do?
Murganah (*coolly*) I would suggest you wear a veil, Princess.

A fanfare

Nouronnihar Oh, no. People are coming. They can't see me like this...

Nouronnihar rushes off as the Sultan enters excitedly. He is followed by the Vizier, Salim and Ali

Sultan Ahmed has returned. He has been sighted from the gates. Ahmed's returned, Murganah.
Murganah (*incredulously*) Ahmed?
Sultan Isn't it the most wonderful news? A feast! I must order a feast...
Ali (*indicating*) Father...
Sultan Mmm?

Ahmed enters. He is dressed in splendid new robes

Murganah draws on her veil

Ahmed Father.
Sultan (*moved*) Ahmed!

They embrace. Ahmed then embraces Ali

Ahmed Ali! So good to see you all!
Ali Ahmed! Where have you been?
Ahmed All in good time. (*He looks at Murganah*) Murganah? Is that you?
Murganah (*curtsying*) Your Highness.
Ahmed I'm home.
Murganah I am delighted, your Highness.
Ahmed Murganah, it's me. Ahmed.
Murganah Your Highness.
Ahmed (*a little confused by her coolness*) Where's my big brother? Where's Houssain?
Sultan He—he went away, Ahmed. When we thought you were dead, Houssain decided to retire with his books. We've not seen or heard from him.
Ahmed But I'm alive. Now he can return.
Ali He's gone to some remote place, heaven knows where.
Ahmed Oh. Well, we must find him. My Lord Grand Vizier. I apologise for not greeting you sooner.

Muffled sounds from the Vizier. Ahmed looks puzzled

Sultan The Grand Vizier has—developed some speech problems of late.
Ahmed Oh dear. I'm sorry to hear that.

Muffled sounds from the Vizier

Special Emissary Salim! Greetings!
Salim (*singing, loudly*) I ride along the mountain trail on the Road to Samarkand...

The Sultan hits him. Salim stops abruptly

Ahmed (*puzzled*) I'm sorry?
Sultan Take no notice. He's completely deranged. We still await the instruction booklet to repair him.
Ahmed I see. And the Princess Nouronnihar? She is well?
Ali Yes, she is—she is... She is now my wife.

Ahmed You're married!
Sultan Where is she? She should be here. Summon the Princess!

Murganah goes off to fetch her

Ahmed Ali, I'm so thrilled for you! Are you happy, you lucky man? Is she as beautiful as ever?
Ali Yes, well, she's... Tell us about yourself, Ahmed.
Sultan Yes. Where have you been, boy? Where did you obtain these splendid clothes? Not from the top of a mountain, surely?
Ahmed Father, it is very awkward but I have been sworn to secrecy.
Sultan Secrecy? By whom?
Ahmed That's a secret, I'm afraid.
Sultan Nonsense! He's met some woman. That's what it is. We'll soon get it out of you, boy. Get you drunk over a good feast...
Ahmed Nor can I stay here more than an hour. I have been sworn to that as well.
Sultan What is all this about? Swearing this and swearing that...?

Murganah enters with Nouronnihar who is now swathed in veils

Murganah Her Royal Highness The Princess Nouronnihar.
Ahmed (*turning to greet her*) Princess Nouronn... (*He stops at the sight of her*) Princess?
Nouronnihar (*curtsying awkwardly, muffled*) My Lord...
Ahmed (*to Ali*) Why is she wrapped up like that?
Ali She—she——
Murganah It is the custom in the Princess's own country to save her radiant beauty for her husband's eyes alone...

A muffled moan from Nouronnihar

Ahmed I see. Well. Lucky man, Ali.
Ali (*unhappily*) Yes.
Ahmed And unless I am very much mistaken the Princess is shortly expecting a happy event?

Another moan from Nouronnihar

Ali No. No happy events.
Ahmed No? I'm sorry.
Ali Not a single one.

Nouronnihar rushes out, weeping

Sultan Come! Let us go indoors. At least we shall give you a breakfast feast, if nothing else. Everyone inside! Grand Vizier, write it to the kitchens. I want a breakfast feast for three hundred at once.

The Sultan and the Vizier go off

Salim (*as he goes, singing, loudly*) I ride along the mountain trail on the Road to Samarkand...

Salim exits

Ali Coming, brother?
Ahmed (*with a glance at Murganah*) Just one moment, Ali. I'll follow.
Ali (*reluctantly going*) This is all in your honour, you know. Don't be long.

Ali exits

Ahmed is left alone with Murganah

Ahmed I may be wrong but I sense that in one area at least I am not welcome back at all.
Murganah Why should you think that?
Ahmed From your attitude towards me. It seems almost hostile.
Murganah Perhaps there's good reason.
Ahmed Why? What have I done?
Murganah Tell me.
Ahmed I can't begin to think.
Murganah You go away—for weeks. We presume you dead. Not a word. Then you return like some glorious prodigal son. Dressed like a—like a king and tell us nothing. That you've been sworn to secrecy.
Ahmed It's the truth.
Murganah Who is she?
Ahmed I can't tell you.
Murganah Then it is a woman?
Ahmed Possibly. Possibly not. How do you know?
Murganah Because you didn't choose those clothes yourself. That took a woman's eye. A woman moreover who loves you.
Ahmed Rubbish.
Murganah And I only have to look in your eyes to see that that love is reciprocated.
Ahmed You don't know this. How could you possibly know this?
Murganah (*violently*) Because I too am a woman, Ahmed. A woman who loved you, who would have readily died for you, who swore her life away for you. And you have betrayed me. And I will have lived for nothing.

Ahmed (*alarmed*) Murganah!

Murganah And I promise, Ahmed. I will kill you and I will kill her. And before I have finished I will bring down this whole kingdom. I will reduce it to ashes.

Ahmed (*moving to her and attempting to touch her*) Please listen to me…

Murganah Don't touch me! Don't ever touch me again! (*She produces a dagger and strikes at Ahmed*)

Ahmed manages to fend off the blow. But in the ensuing brief struggle Murganah easily overpowers Ahmed and holds the dagger to his throat

(*Laughing*) You could never beat me, could you, Ahmed? And you never will. And one day when I choose to do so, I will kill you as easily as this.

A second and she releases him. Ahmed realizes he has been within an inch of death

The Sultan enters

Murganah steps back and hides the dagger

Sultan Come along! We're all in there, waiting for you, Ahmed! Come on, boy, if you've only an hour then at least spend it with us.

Ahmed (*very upset*) I'm sorry, Father. I cannot stop for a feast. I have no time. I'm sorry.

Sultan Can't stop? You mean we've got to cancel it?

Ahmed goes

The Sultan is about to follow him

Murganah My Lord…

Sultan Yes? Ah, Murganah…

Murganah May I have your permission to speak, sire.

Sultan Of course, only I'm just——

Murganah I will be brief, sire. I do not wish to alarm you but I believe the Prince's secrecy regarding his absence may have sinister implications for us all.

Sultan What on earth do you mean?

Murganah I will speak frankly. The Prince Ahmed is a dear friend. I would not wish him harm. But he is impressionable and easily swayed by unscrupulous people. He is a truly honest and honourable man and sadly men such as those are often the most easily led, for they trust everyone.

Sultan This is true. Only too true.

Murganah I think, even now, the Prince may have fallen under a wrong influence. One that means not only harm to him but to this whole kingdom.

Sultan You really think so?

Murganah There is something evil at work here. I sense it. I fear for him; I fear for you.

Sultan If you are correct, what are we to do?

Murganah Sire, when he leaves allow me to follow him.

Sultan You?

Murganah Please, sire...

Sultan But Murganah, this could prove dangerous, you're only a——

Murganah I am only a humble servant, sire, I know. But that is also my strength. I will pass unnoticed. One servant more or less. Who would know?

Sultan You're much more than a mere servant, Murganah, believe me. Very well. As soon as you find where he's gone, return at once and report to me personally. And to no-one else.

Murganah Thank you, sire.

Sultan (*as he goes*) Murganah!

Murganah Sire?

Sultan Take care, won't you? I think you're rather—special. Hate to lose you.

Murganah Thank you, sire.

The Sultan goes

Murganah, pleased, prepares to leave

Ali enters

Ali Murganah...

Murganah (*irritably*) What do you want?

Ali I saw you there with Ahmed. Does that mean it's all over between us, now he's back?

Murganah What's all over?

Ali You're back with him again. Is that it? If so, what about me?

Murganah I am not back with anyone. I am free. As I've always been. I am not with him as you put it. And I am certainly not with you. Now leave me alone!

Ali Murganah, you can't do this. What am I going to do?

Murganah I suggest you go and try and cheer up your wife.

Ali (*in desperation*) My wife? I don't want to be with my wife. I want to be with you. I don't love my wife, I've told you. I can't stand the sight of her. I can't even bear to look at her.

Murganah (*in sudden anger*) Then don't! (*She gives a sudden violent gesture stabbing her fingers towards Ali's face*) And stop staring at me!

Ali gives a cry and clutches his face

Ali My eyes! What have you done to my eyes? Murganah! I'm blind! Murganah!

Murganah has gone

Ali staggers off calling her name as he goes. As he does this, the scene changes

SCENE 11

The Mountain of Storms

The weather is as wild as ever

Ahmed enters, making his way to the top

Ahmed How am I ever going to find my way back in this? It's impossible. (*He climbs a little further. He hears something below him and turns*) Who is that? Is someone there? Is that someone following me? Come out, whoever you are?

Murganah appears

Murganah, what are you doing here?
Murganah Ahmed, I'm sorry.
Ahmed I thought you never wanted to see me again. I thought you'd sworn to kill me.
Murganah I'm sorry. Forgive me.
Ahmed I do. I do forgive you. Now go back. Before you freeze to death. Go home.
Murganah I must come with you.
Ahmed Well, you can't. Now go back...
Murganah Ahmed!
Ahmed Go back! Back! (*He starts on up the mountain*)

Murganah stares after him, then contrives a fairly spectacular fall, crying out as she does so

(*Turning back to her, alarmed*) Murganah! (*He scrambles back down to her*)

She is moaning in pain

Are you all right?
Murganah (*moaning*) My leg! My leg!
Ahmed (*trying to help her up*) Can you stand?
Murganah (*crying with pain*) Aaaah! I think it may be broken.
Ahmed Oh, Lord! Here! (*He lifts her and starts to carry her up the mountain*) There's the palace! We're nearly there!

As they continue up, the scene changes

SCENE 12

Paribanou's Mountain Palace

Ahmed enters, still carrying Murganah

Ahmed (*calling*) Nasuh! Nasuh!

Nasuh enters swiftly

Quickly, help me with her!
Nasuh Why have you brought her back here?
Ahmed I couldn't leave her there on the mountain, she would have died. Quickly, put her on the couch.

Nasuh reluctantly takes Murganah from Ahmed and lays her on the couch. As he does this, Paribanou enters

Paribanou What's happening? What is this?
Ahmed I'm sorry, she's a friend. She followed me. She's hurt. I couldn't leave her to die. How is she?

Murganah groans and appears to recover

Nasuh She's coming round.
Murganah (*weakly*) Where am I…? Where…? (*She sees Paribanou*)

They stare at each other for a moment

I know you.

Paribanou And I you.

Ahmed You've met before? How marvellous!

Paribanou Have done. Or will do. Are you injured?

Ahmed Her leg. She's hurt her leg. She thinks it may be broken.

Paribanou Oh, I'm so sorry. May I see? (*She moves to Murganah*)

Murganah (*drawing back, warily*) No! It's fine. It was probably just a sprain.

Paribanou If I could just——

Murganah I'd sooner you didn't touch me. Please.

Paribanou (*smiling*) As you wish.

Murganah I will leave. I sense I am not welcome here. (*She gets up, limping only slightly*)

Ahmed Murganah, wait! You can't leave yet.

Murganah (*to Paribanou*) Thank you for your hospitality. Fascinating to—recognize you again.

Ahmed Please. One minute. Paribanou, ask her to stay.

Paribanou Your friend apparently wishes to leave. Why should I stop her?

Ahmed Please, Murganah. One minute. Wait one minute. Please.

Murganah (*moving to the door*) I'll wait out here.

Paribanou Nasuh! Keep our guest company.

Nasuh (*grimly*) I will.

Nasuh goes off with Murganah

Ahmed What is all this? Have you both really met before?

Paribanou Not as such.

Ahmed I don't understand.

Paribanou Ahmed, she may have been your friend once but she has changed. Murganah has surely altered since you first knew her. She is now a very dangerous person. I beg you, have nothing more to do with her.

Ahmed What are you saying?

Paribanou Do you love her?

Ahmed I am—deeply, deeply fond of her.

Paribanou But not love?

Ahmed (*angrily*) I don't know. All I know is Murganah is my friend and I will stand by her. And if you intend throwing her out, then I must go too.

Paribanou Ahmed! Listen——

Ahmed No, I'm sorry. Champion or no, there is such a thing as loyalty. She is my sworn blood twin. I will stand by her. I couldn't leave her to make that journey back on her own. What sort of friend would I be then? (*He starts to go*)

Paribanou Listen to me! Ahmed! Come back here!

Ahmed has gone

Paribanou looks worried

In a second, Nasuh enters with a small glass jar

They've both gone?
Nasuh They've gone. I fear we may never see him again.
Paribanou Maybe.
Nasuh She—your visitor left you a small gift.
Paribanou What is it?
Nasuh (*examining the jar*) Oranges, they look like.
Paribanou (*taking them from him*) How considerate of her. (*She holds the jar in her hands*)
Nasuh Lady, I would advise you not to eat——

The jar turns suddenly into a small bunch of flowers

Paribanou (*handing them back to Nasuh*) Put them in water for me, would you, Nasuh?

Nasuh goes off. Paribanou follows. As they go, the scene changes

SCENE 13

The Mountain of Storms

The wind is howling as usual

Ahmed enters, helping Murganah down the mountain side

Ahmed Come on! Put your foot there, that's it. You're doing well.
Murganah (*triumphantly gripping his hand*) You chose rightly, Ahmed. Well done!
Ahmed How do you mean?
Murganah You chose me, not her. I knew you wouldn't desert me. I knew you wouldn't.
Ahmed Of course I wouldn't.
Murganah And it's me you love?
Ahmed (*pretending not to hear above the wind*) What?
Murganah I said, it's me you love. Tell me it's me you love. Not her?
Ahmed Who? Paribanou? What makes you think I love her?

Murganah Then tell me you don't. Say you don't love her.
Ahmed Look, this is hardly the place, is it?
Murganah Say it!
Ahmed Can't we wait till we...?
Murganah (*fiercely*) Say it!

Ahmed is silent

You can't, can you? You can't say it? (*She screams above the wind*) You
can't say it?
Ahmed I don't know. I just——
Murganah Then go back to her! Go on! But I warn you, you won't find her
quite so pretty as when you left her. I promise you that.
Ahmed What have you done? What have you done to her?
Murganah Go back! See for yourself!
Ahmed If you've done anything to hurt her...! I'll——
Murganah You'll what?
Ahmed All right, I love her! Is that good enough for you! I do. I love her!
(*He starts back up the mountain*)
Murganah Then die for love, then! Stay here and die! Die!

*As Murganah moves away, there is a great rumbling as of an avalanche.
Ahmed throws up his arms in alarm. He cries out as the avalanche strikes him
and he is bowled over on to his face*

Murganah has gone

Ahmed lies very still. The avalanche has passed

*In a moment, a figure, tall and angular, arrives. We dimly recognize that
it is Houssain. He bends over Ahmed*

Houssain (*above the storm*) I say, are you all right?

*Ahmed does not move. With an effort, Houssain moves some rocks which are
trapping Ahmed's body. He turns Ahmed over*

Ahmed! Ahmed!

Houssain starts to drag Ahmed clear. As he does this, we find ourselves in

SCENE 14

Houssain's Hut

It is filled with books. Indeed, there is very little room for much else. Simple and spartan as befits a hermit

Houssain drags Ahmed into the middle of the room. He closes the door. The wind stops abruptly

Houssain (*to himself*) There. Get you in the warm. Freezing out there. (*He bends over his brother*) Ahmed! Ahmed!

Ahmed groans

Oh, thank heaven.
Ahmed Houssain! How did you...?
Houssain I found you. You were trapped by an avalanche. You're lucky I did. This is a deserted spot. I only went out for some firewood. Always forgetting to get it in. How do you feel? Are you all right?
Ahmed (*flexing his legs and trying to stand*) Yes, I think... I should be...
Houssain Careful. Don't try and do too much straightaway. Sit down there. I'll get you some coffee. I make it with pine cones. It's very good. Wait there. There's always some on the boil.

Houssain goes off

Ahmed looks around

Ahmed (*calling to Houssain*) What is this place?
Houssain (*off*) It's my new home. Used to be a foresters' hut. Two rooms. This one and that one. Just enough for me and all my beautiful books.
Ahmed I've noticed them. (*He opens a book at random*)

Something pops its head out and disappears immediately. Ahmed jumps in alarm

What on earth was that?
Houssain What?
Ahmed There's something in one of these books. An animal of some sort.

Houssain enters with a dirty chipped mug

Houssain Ah, that'll be Omar.

Ahmed Omar?

Houssain I named him that. I found him in one of the books. He's a Bookmarker.

Ahmed A Bookmarker?

Houssain I bought a load of books off a merchant from Samarkand. He threw in Omar. He's very handy. Eats a little waste paper, sleeps most of the time between the pages of your book and marks your place in the process. Here... (*He hands the mug to Ahmed. Coaxingly*) Omar! Come on, Omar! Come and say hallo! Omar!

Omar pops his head out of the book

This is Ahmed, Omar! He's my kid brother. Ahmed, say hallo to Omar.

Ahmed (*extending his hand, uncertainly*) Hallo!

Omar gives a squeak and disappears

Houssain No, he's very shy. When I first got him it took months before he'd come out of the dictionary. How's the coffee?

Ahmed (*trying it, with ill disguised distaste*) Ah! Very. Interesting.

Houssain Come on then!

Ahmed What?

Houssain Bed. You can have my bed.

Ahmed But I have to get back——

Houssain Not tonight you don't.

Ahmed (*spilling out his fears*) Houssain, you don't understand. If I don't get back to her I fear that someone who is very—dear—to me, is in terrible danger. I don't know what I'm going to do, Houssain. I really don't.

Houssain Who are you talking about? Murganah?

Ahmed No! Not Murganah. Certainly not Murganah! Someone else.

Houssain My brothers and their women, really!

Ahmed I promised I would be her Champion, you see. Fight on her behalf. But you know me, Houssain. I'm no Champion. I'm hopeless, I can barely lift a sword. And now I think I know who it is she wants me to fight. And I'm not sure I can do it, Houssain. And even if I could, I'm not sure I could win. In fact I know I couldn't win. There's no way I could win against——

Houssain (*gently, under the last*) Ahmed! Ahmed! Ahmed!

Ahmed What?

Houssain Slow down. Please. Now listen. I have not been a good older brother to you in the past, I know. I could have been more help if I had chosen. Instead, I have selfishly stayed in my books in my own private world...

Ahmed No, you've not, you've been——

Houssain Listen. I too am no fighter. But I do know things about fighting. We need to talk. It's been long overdue——
Ahmed But what about...?
Houssain But first sleep. You can return to your friend in the morning after we've talked. In fact, we can talk on the way. Come on. Big brother's telling you. Bed! You can hardly stand.
Ahmed (*sighing*) All right!
Houssain (*as they go*) It's an interesting bed. I made it myself. Pine needles and then a layer of bracken. Very comfortable.
Ahmed (*alarmed*) Pine needles?

As Ahmed and Houssain go out, the scene changes

SCENE 15

The Sultan's Palace

Murganah enters

She is dressed resplendently, no longer bothering to maintain her role as a servant

Murganah (*yelling*) I said I wanted everyone assembled here at once! Where are you? Where are you?

The pathetic survivors of the palace come on. The speechless Grand Vizier, the blind Ali led by a fat, totally cocooned Nouronnihar. Finally Salim, looking terribly the worse for wear

They all stand reverently

Salim (*singing*) All hail the Princess, our lovely Princess. We love our Princess. Long may she live.
Murganah Is this all of you? Is this all there are? (*She pauses*) Somebody answer me. Quickly, I warn you.

The Vizier makes muffled sounds

Ali This is all of us, I believe.
Murganah All of us—who?
Ali All of us, Princess.
Nouronnihar (*meekly*) All of us who can still move, Princess. If you will remember you lost your temper with the Palace Guard and——

Murganah I know what I did, thank you. I don't need reminding by you, you gross chimpanzee.

The Sultan hurries on

Where have you been?

Sultan I'm so sorry, Princess. I had important matters to deal with——

Murganah Let us get one thing straight, shall we? When I give an order, there is nothing—nothing more important than that order. Do you understand that?

Sultan Yes. It was a matter of settling the budget for the——

Murganah (*yelling*) DO YOU UNDERSTAND THAT?

Sultan (*meekly*) Yes, Princess.

Murganah Then in future you do as you're told, you dismal old bat!

Sultan Now, now, now. Really! I must ask you not to—not to—talk to me in that tone. I am—I am—the Sultan—and as such I am owed a certain— I am your senior. You must surely respect your elders. Show some respect for age.

Murganah Age? You believe age gives you privilege? Automatic rights?

Sultan Well, surely...

Murganah And you demand those rights, do you?

Sultan I think it's generally understood that——

Murganah (*stretching out her hand as before*) Then if you value age so much, I'll give you it.

As she speaks the Sultan ages visibly in front of her

Age then, old man. Age and age and—age.

The Sultan becomes a shrunken, helpless old man. The others stand by powerless

Nouronnihar No...

Murganah Be quiet, chimp! Come along! We've all got duties to perform, haven't we? Then let's get on with them.

They all move off

Salim (*singing*) All hail the Princess, our lovely——

Murganah (*as she goes*) Shut up!

As they all go off, the scene fades to

SCENE 16

Paribanou's Mountain Palace

Paribanou is standing sadly

In a moment, Nasuh enters

Nasuh Lady, he has returned. Ahmed has returned.
Paribanou (*overjoyed*) He's alive?
Nasuh Alive and well. His brother found him and saved his life. The woman had left him on the mountain for dead.
Paribanou Oh, heaven be praised!

Ahmed appears in the doorway with Houssain behind him

Paribanou looks at him for a second. They move and embrace each other. After a second they break apart, somewhat embarrassed

(*In confusion*) I'm sorry, I——
Ahmed (*equally flustered*) No, I'm—sorry I... I was——
Paribanou ...pleased to see you...
Ahmed ...glad you were not... I was frightened you might...
Paribanou ...that you were... Oh!
Ahmed Oh!

They embrace again. They part

Paribanou ⎱
            ⎰ (*together; apologetically, to the others*) Sorry!
Ahmed
Houssain I take it you two know each other?
Ahmed (*laughing nervously*) Yes. I just wanted to tell you both that in the brief time I've been away—I know it hasn't been long—I have learnt certain things. One of those is that occasionally one must stand up and fight. Not always with swords but at the very least with words and thoughts. But if it comes to swords, then...
Houssain If it does come to swords, I have taught him a valuable lesson...
Nasuh *You* have taught him a lesson? To do with swords?
Ahmed Yes, Houssain has taught me the most important thing, Nasuh. To believe in myself. To believe that I can win.
Nasuh (*unconvinced*) We shall see.
Ahmed Try me.
Houssain Ahmed, be careful, you're still weak.

Ahmed Come on, Nasuh! Try me!
Nasuh Very well. (*He goes for the swords*)
Paribanou Be careful, Ahmed. Being over-confident is almost as——
Ahmed Don't worry.

Nasuh has fetched the swords. Ahmed now takes his

Nasuh Are you ready?
Ahmed Ready.

Ahmed and Nasuh fight. For a second it is evenly matched but suddenly Ahmed finds an opening and for the first time has Nasuh at his mercy. Nasuh is amazed

Houssain Bravo!
Paribanou (*somewhat incredulously*) Bravo, indeed. Bravo!
Ahmed Am I a worthy Champion?
Paribanou Truly you are. Only I, too, have learnt a lesson whilst you've been away.
Ahmed What's that?
Paribanou That I wish it were someone other than you that has to fight. It would break my heart if anything happened to you.
Ahmed Then I must make sure that I come back, mustn't I? (*As he goes off*) Come on, Nasuh, let's practise.

Ahmed goes off

Nasuh looks at Paribanou

Paribanou Teach him well, Nasuh.
Nasuh I'll do my best. There's little left I can teach him, I'm afraid.
Paribanou (*excitedly*) He did beat you, didn't he? He actually beat you.
Nasuh Me, yes. But I am not Murganah.

Nasuh goes

Paribanou looks worriedly at Houssain

Houssain Keep faith.
Paribanou Yes.
Houssain He needs our faith.

Paribanou and Houssain go out as the scene changes

SCENE 17

The Sultan's Palace. It is dawn

A great hammering on the gates

Ali comes on with Nouronnihar leading him, as before

Ali What's happening? What's the noise?
Nouronnihar It's someone at the gates. Somebody said it was Ahmed.
Ali Ahmed? She told us he was dead.
Nouronnihar Apparently he isn't. And Houssain's with him as well.
Ali What are they both doing here, the fools?
Nouronnihar Maybe they've come back to save us?
Ali Oh, yes. Very likely. An intellectual who barely has the strength to lift a pen and a coward with his head in the clouds. Very likely.

More banging

  Murganah enters angrily

Murganah What is that noise? Who's woken me with that noise?
Ali It wasn't us, Princess.
Murganah I know it wasn't you, you fool. You're standing there. Who is it? Vizier! (*She yells*) Vizier! I thought I put Salim at the gates to drive people away. (*She yells*) Salim!
Nouronnihar Salim has finally broken down, Princess.
Murganah Broken?
Nouronnihar (*weeping*) You made him stand out in the rain and he fell apart.
Murganah Shut up, shut up, shut up!

  The Vizier enters, apparently still struggling into his clothes

Vizier! Find out who that is, at once.

  The Vizier hurries off

If there's one thing guaranteed to put me in a bad temper, it's being woken up from a sound sleep!
Ali Oh!
Nouronnihar Oh!
Murganah Be quiet!

  The Sultan enters. He is now very frail

Sultan It is rumoured, Princess, that it is Ahmed at the door.
Murganah What did you say? Did you say Ahmed?
Sultan Ahmed. And his brother Houssain.
Murganah You're senile, you stupid old man.
Sultan No, no, definitely Ahmed. Some people told me.

The Vizier enters hastily

Murganah Is it Ahmed?

The Vizier nods

Well, well, well. So he returns. Ahmed returns. We must welcome him
then, mustn't we? Open the gates. (*She yells*) Open the gates.

Murganah goes off

A fanfare

*Ahmed comes on dressed for a fight. He has his helmet and sword. Behind
him comes Houssain*

Ali Who is it? Who's coming?
Nouronnihar It's Ahmed and Houssain.
Ali The fools! Why have they come here? Get away. Tell them to get away
from here!

The fanfare stops. A silence

Houssain (*looking at them all*) What has been happening here? Father?
Sultan Terrible things, my son. Too terrible to mention.
Houssain I cannot believe what I'm seeing. Ali?
Ali Houssain? Is that you?
Nouronnihar Yes, it's Houssain, Ali.
Houssain (*incredulously*) Nouronnihar?
Nouronnihar Yes.
Houssain Princess Nouronnihar?
Nouronnihar (*alarmed*) No, no! Not Princess. I am not Princess. Please
don't call me Princess. There is only one Princess now. She who rules us
all.
Ali And who will now rule you.
Houssain You mean Murganah? Are you talking of Murganah?

Another fanfare, menacing and bigger than before

*Murganah enters. She is now in her fighting clothes and carries her helmet
and sword*

All but Ahmed and Houssain kneel as she enters

Murganah (*nodding*) Ahmed.
Ahmed Murganah.
Murganah I see you and your brother no longer have the breeding to bow
or kneel before a Princess.
Ahmed We prefer to choose whom we kneel before.
Murganah I should value that choice whilst you have it. Why have you come
here?
Ahmed I am the Champion of Paribanou who is your sworn enemy and rival.
On her behalf I am here to fight you. And if necessary kill you.
Murganah (*laughing*) Big speeches. Big words.
Ahmed I am prepared to back them up.
Murganah I could melt that sword in your hand without moving a muscle.
I could wither your arms and crumble the very bones in your legs. What
sort of fight would that be?
Ahmed It would prove nothing, of course. Except that you lack the courage
to fight me fairly and squarely. Without recourse to tricks.
Murganah You think I couldn't?
Ahmed I believe you may be frightened.
Murganah Frightened? Ahmed, we've known each other since we were
children. I've always beaten you. Always. I beat you with sticks and later
I beat you with swords. Why should things change? Put down your weapon
and kneel and we'll forget it.
Ahmed I prefer to fight.
Murganah Then you're a fool. I will tell you this. I shall not enjoy killing
you, Ahmed. I loved you but you scorned that love. You threw it back in
my face. Not once but twice. Once with her—(*she indicates Nouronnihar*)
—and once with your so called Lady—Paribanou.
Ahmed I have behaved honourably.
Murganah (*angrily*) Well, I don't think you have.
Ahmed I behaved as my duty dictated that I should——
Murganah You've behaved like a traitor! A traitor to me! And you will die
like a traitor! Very well. Let's finish this. I'm sorry. You leave me no
choice.
Houssain (*softly to Ahmed*) Good. She's angry. It's good to get her angry.
Ahmed (*worried*) Good for who?

*They prepare to fight. Both put on their fighting helmets, versions of the
earlier ones but more ornate. A drum beats. The spectators rise and draw*

back to the edges of the area to form an arena. The fight begins. Evenly matched at first, Murganah is obviously a little taken aback at Ahmed's new found prowess

Murganah Good, Ahmed! Good!

Ahmed, encouraged, almost makes a fatal slip

(*Laughing*) Oh, Ahmed. To fall for that. You always used to fall for that. (*She prepares for the* coup de grâce)

Ahmed somehow wriggles free. The fight see-saws back and forth becoming more serious, more keenly contested. At last Murganah appears to have the upper hand once again. But a burst of overconfidence proves her final undoing. Ahmed stabs her. She stares at him incredulously. Her sword slips from her hand and she slowly drops to the floor

Oh, Ahmed. What have you done?
Ahmed (*kneeling by her*) Murganah. I will fetch a doctor. Maybe he can...
Murganah (*her voice growing weaker*) No, Ahmed. You've done for me ... done for me. Even in death, I still love you. I'm sorry...

A strange sound is heard as the room grows darker and eerier

A cowled dark figure appears. It is Schaibar, returned for Murganah, as he promised

Everyone, including Ahmed, draws back

Schaibar... Schaibar...

Schaibar reaches Murganah. He slides back his hood to reveal the face of Death

Schaibar (*softly*) Murganah, I have come for you at last. Take my hand, child.
Murganah (*taking his hand*) Schaibar...
Schaibar Come with me now. And I will give you peace. Come now. Come.

Schaibar leads Murganah away

The sounds fade and the Light brightens

Ahmed (*recovering first*) She's gone.

Ali Yes, I know, I saw it. (*He realizes*) I saw it! I saw it.
Nouronnihar Ali, you can see?
Ali I can see.
Vizier Praise be to heaven! (*He realizes*) Praise be to heaven! Praise be to heaven! (*He laughs*)
Sultan Well fought, lad. Damn good fight. Didn't know you had it in you!
Ahmed Thank you, Father.
Sultan I feel better as well. Twenty years younger.
Ali Oh, Nouronnihar! Forgive me. (*He reaches for her*)
Nouronnihar (*drawing away*) No, no. Please...
Ali Come on! Take off that veil, I want to look at my wife...
Nouronnihar (*desperately*) Please, don't. Please, I beg you.

Ali has grasped the edge of her veil. As she steps back the whole of her outer garment pulls away to reveal the former Nouronnihar

Oh! Oh, goodness!
Ali Oh, my beautiful Princess!
Nouronnihar Oh, my lovely husband!

They embrace

Sultan Very well. In honour of your victory, a feast! Grand Vizier. Tell the kitchens to prepare a banquet for a thousand. In honour of my gallant son, Prince Ahmed.
Vizier But, sire, the cooks. We have no cooks.
Sultan No cooks.
Vizier She exiled the cooks.
Sultan (*appalled*) No cooks? What are we going to do? Do something at once!

The Vizier goes off briefly

Ahmed Father, in any case I cannot stay. I'm sorry.
Sultan Can't stay? Why ever not?
Ahmed I am the Champion of Paribanou. I must return to her and set her free.

Paribanou appears with Nasuh

Paribanou No need, I am here. You have already set me free. And I in turn release you from your vow to me, if you so wish.
Ahmed For as long as you will permit me, lady, I will remain your Champion.

Paribanou (*smiling*) Very well. But I should warn you. It will be for ever.
Sultan Now what about these cooks? Who's going to cook?

The Vizier enters

Vizier Sire, good news! A cook has been found!
Sultan Splendid. Come on, everybody!
Houssain Not me, Father, I'm sorry I do have to get back to my books.
Ali No, you don't, you're staying.
Ahmed You're staying!
Nouronnihar You're staying!
Houssain I'm staying.
Sultan Everyone's staying! At last, a feast! Ahmed, lead us in!
Ahmed (*proffering his arm*) Would you do me the honour, my lady!
Paribanou The honour is mine, Sir Champion...

Music as they start to process inside

Salim appears in the doorway. He is more or less reassembled. He has on a chef's hat and holds a covered dish

Salim (*proudly*) Served is dinner! (*He lifts the cover on the dish and is enveloped with smoke*)

They all laugh and go off to more music

Black-out

FURNITURE AND PROPERTY LIST

Further dressing may be added at the director's discretion

ACT I

SCENE 1

On stage: SULTAN'S PALACE GROUNDS:
          Tree

Off stage: Book (**Houssain**)
          Practice sword (**Ahmed**)
          Practice sword (**Murganah**)

Personal: **Ahmed:** protective helmet
          Murganah: protective helmet

SCENE 2

On stage: GRAND DRAWING-ROOM IN SULTAN'S PALACE:
          Houssain's book

Personal: **Ahmed:** jacket
          Nouronnihar: veil (worn throughout)
          Safia: veil (worn throughout)
          Murganah: veil (worn throughout)
          Salim: sword (carried throughout)

SCENE 3

On stage: SULTAN'S PALACE COURTYARD

SCENE 4

On stage: THE INN:
          Tables. *On one table*: game of patience with tarot cards
          Chairs

Off stage: Tankard of ale **(Innkeeper)**
Sword **(Murganah)**
Glass of wine **(Nouronnihar)**
Two tankards on tray **(Innkeeper)**

Personal: **Highwayman:** long knife
Ahmed: purse with money
Murganah: mask
Schaibar: black star stamp

SCENE 5

On stage: THE INN

Off stage: Carpet **(Houssain)**
Telescope **(Ali)**
Four glasses of ale on tray **(Innkeeper)**

Personal: **Ahmed:** apple

SCENE 6

On stage: NOURONNIHAR'S BEDSIDE:
Bed

Personal: **Ahmed:** apple

SCENE 7

On stage: AT THE FOOT OF THE MOUNTAIN OF STORMS

Off stage: Long bow, arrows**(Vizier)**

SCENE 8

On stage: NEAR THE SUMMIT OF THE MOUNTAIN OF STORMS

ACT II

SCENE 1

On stage: PARIBANOU'S MOUNTAIN PALACE:
Torch

Jewels
Couch

SCENE 2

On stage: SULTAN'S PALACE

Personal: **Murganah:** small ornamental jar

SCENE 3

On stage: PARIBANOU'S MOUNTAIN PALACE

SCENE 4

On stage: SULTAN'S PALACE

Personal: **Murganah:** small ornamental jar
               Salim: removable arm

SCENE 5

On stage: PARIBANOU'S MOUNTAIN PALACE

Off stage: Sword (**Ahmed**)
               Sword (**Nasuh**)

SCENE 6

On stage: SULTAN'S PALACE

Off stage: Goblet of wine (**Murganah**)

Personal: **Salim:** loose chunk of him

SCENE 7

On stage: PARIBANOU'S MOUNTAIN PALACE

Off stage: Sword (**Ahmed**)
               Sword (**Nasuh**)

SCENE 8

On stage: SULTAN'S PALACE GARDENS

Personal: **Murganah:** small jar of cream

SCENE 9

On stage: PARIBANOU'S MOUNTAIN PALACE

SCENE 10

On stage: SULTAN'S PALACE GARDENS

Personal: **Murganah:** dagger

SCENE 11

On stage: MOUNTAIN OF STORMS

SCENE 12

On stage: PARIBANOU'S MOUNTAIN PALACE

Off stage: Small glass jar/bunch of flowers (**Nasuh**)

SCENE 13

On stage: MOUNTAIN OF STORMS
              Avalanche matter

SCENE 14

On stage: HOUSSAIN'S HUT
              Books
              Book with pop-up creature Omar

Off stage: Dirty chipped mug of coffee (**Houssain**)

SCENE 15

On stage: SULTAN'S PALACE

SCENE 16

On stage: PARIBANOU'S MOUNTAIN PALACE
              Swords

SCENE 17

On stage: SULTAN'S PALACE

Off stage: Ornate helmet, sword (**Ahmed**)
              Ornate helmet, sword (**Murganah**)
              Covered dish containing dry ice (**Salim**)

Personal: **Salim:** chef's hat

LIGHTING PLOT

Property fittings required: torch
Various interior and exterior settings

ACT I, SCENE 1

To open: Overall general lighting

No cues

ACT I, SCENE 2

To open: Overall general lighting

No cues

ACT I, SCENE 3

To open: Night-time lighting

Cue 1   **Houssain**: "Let's get the horses..."   (Page 15)
         Turn on light in a window

ACT I, SCENE 4

To open: Overall general lighting

Cue 2   **Schaibar** makes a pass with his hand   (Page 21)
         Weak spot on **Ahmed**

Cue 3   **Ahmed** finds his way   (Page 21)
         Fade out spot on **Ahmed**

| *Cue* 4 | **Murganah** waves her hand
Weak spot on **Nouronnihar** | (Page 23) |

| *Cue* 5 | **Murganah** laughs with delight
Fade out spot on **Nouronnihar** | (Page 23) |

ACT I, SCENE 5

To open: Bright sunny morning lighting

| *Cue* 6 | **The brothers** start flying journey
Fade lights on **Innkeeper** *and* **Murganah** | (Page 29) |

ACT I, SCENE 6

To open: Overall general lighting

No cues

ACT I, SCENE 7

To open: Overall general lighting

No cues

ACT I, SCENE 8

To open: Bleak storm lighting

| *Cue* 7 | **The wind** increases to a howl
Blizzard effect, continuing | (Page 38) |

| *Cue* 8 | **Nasuh** carries **Ahmed** away
Fade to black-out | (Page 39) |

ACT II, SCENE 1

To open: Torch lighting

ACT II, SCENE 2

To open: Overall general lighting

No cues

ACT II, SCENE 3

To open: Torch lighting

No cues

ACT II, SCENE 4

To open: Overall general lighting

No cues

ACT II, SCENE 5

To open: Torch lighting

No cues

ACT II, SCENE 6

To open: Overall general lighting

No cues

ACT II, SCENE 7

To open: Torch lighting

No cues

ACT II, Scene 8

To open: Overall general lighting

No cues

ACT II, Scene 9

To open: Torch lighting

No cues

ACT II, Scene 10

To open: Early dawn lighting

No cues

ACT II, Scene 11

To open: Bleak storm lighting

No cues

ACT II, Scene 12

To open: Torch lighting

No cues

ACT II, Scene 13

To open: Bleak storm lighting

No cues

ACT II, Scene 14

To open: Overall general lighting

No cues

ACT II, Scene 15

To open: Overall general lighting

Cue 9   **All** go off   (Page 69)
             Fade out lighting

ACT II, Scene 16

To open: Torch lighting

No cues

ACT II, Scene 17

To open: Dawn lighting

Cue 10   **Murganah**: "I'm sorry…"   (Page 75)
             Fade lights to eerie level

Cue 11   **Schaibar** leads **Murganah** away   (Page 75)
             Brighten lighting

Cue 12   **All** laugh and go off   (Page 77)
             Black-out

EFFECTS PLOT

ACT I

Cue 1   **Ali**: "All three hundred and twenty-seven rooms…"   (Page 7)
Fanfare

Cue 2   **Vizier**: "They're here, they're here!"   (Page 7)
Fanfare

Cue 3   To open Scene 3   (Page 15)
Sound of restless horses

Cue 4   **Nouronnihar** goes in   (Page 16)
Sound of horses departing

Cue 5   To open Scene 8   (Page 38)
Increasing wind effect

Cue 6   **Ahmed**: "…could shoot an arrow to this height."   (Page 38)
Increase wind effect

Cue 7   **Ahmed** climbs a bit further   (Page 38)
Increase wind effect to a howl, continuing

ACT II

Cue 8   To open Scene 4   (Page 45)
Wedding bells

Cue 9   **Ahmed** sails past **Nasuh** and disappears off   (Page 47)
Crash off

Cue 10   To open Scene 6   (Page 48)
Music for a wedding

Cue 11   **Vizier** touches his mouth, startled   (Page 48)
Cut music; fanfare

Cue 12   **Ali** and **Nouronnihar** step forward   (Page 49)
            Music for dancing

Cue 13   **Nouronnihar** screams and runs away   (Page 49)
            Cut music

Cue 14   **Ahmed** is booted offstage   (Page 50)
            Crash off

Cue 15   **Murganah**: "…suggest you wear a veil, Princess." (Page 55)
            Fanfare

Cue 16   To open Scene 11   (Page 61)
            Wild wind effect

Cue 17   To open Scene 13   (Page 64)
            Howling wind effect

Cue 18   **Murganah** moves away   (Page 65)
            Great rumbling of an avalanche

Cue 19   **Houssain** closes the door   (Page 66)
            Cut wind effect

Cue 20   **Murganah** goes off   (Page 73)
            Fanfare

Cue 21   **Ali**: "Tell them to get away from here!"   (Page 73)
            Cut fanfare

Cue 22   **Houssain**: "Are you talking of Murganah?"   (Page 73)
            Fanfare, menacing and bigger than before

Cue 23   **Ahmed** and **Murganah** put on fighting helmets (Page 74)
            Drum beat

Cue 24   **Murganah**: "I'm sorry…"   (Page 75)
            Strange sounds

Cue 25   **Schaibar** leads **Murganah** away   (Page 75)
            Fade strange sounds

Cue 26   **Paribanou**: "The honour is mine, Sir Champion…" (Page 77)
            Music

Cue 27   **All** laugh and go off (Page 77)
         More music

Lightning Source UK Ltd.
Milton Keynes UK
UKOW01f1401310715

256163UK00014B/195/P